LEADING TEAMS FOR NETWORK MARKETING PROFESSIONALS

The Ultimate 9 Steps to Becoming a Virtual Leader, Creating an Extraordinary Team Culture, and Inspiring People to Take Action in 30 Days

JOSE SANCHEZ MACOTT
IRENNE RODRIGUEZ

Contents

Introduction	v
Join Our Community on Facebook	xiii
Also by Jose Sanchez Macott and Irenne Rodriguez	xv
Your Free Gift	xvii
1. What is a Great Virtual Leader in Network Marketing?	1
2. Position Yourself as an Authority	18
3. Launch New Enrollees to the Moon	31
4. Cultivating Great Relationships Virtually and Offline	44
5. Building Team Culture	56
6. How to Use Facebook Group to Manage Your Team	71
7. Organizing And Managing Remote Interactions	86
8. Becoming the Online Merchant	108
9. Social Selling for Your Team	123
Conclusion	137
Leave a Review	143
References	145

© **Copyright Jose Sanchez Macott and Irenne Rodriguez 2022 - All rights reserved. ISBN: 9798353611998**

The content contained within this book may not be reproduced, duplicated, or transmitted without direct written permission from the author or the publisher.

Under no circumstances will any blame or legal responsibility be held against the publisher, or author, for any damages, reparation, or monetary loss due to the information contained within this book. Either directly or indirectly. You are responsible for your own choices, actions, and results.

Legal Notice:

This book is copyright protected. This book is only for personal use. You cannot amend, distribute, sell, use, quote, or paraphrase any part, or the content within this book, without the consent of the author or publisher.

Disclaimer Notice:

Please note the information contained within this document is for educational and entertainment purposes only. All effort has been executed to present accurate, up-to-date, and reliable, complete information. No warranties of any kind are declared or implied. Readers acknowledge that the author is not engaging in the rendering of legal, financial, medical, or professional advice. The content within this book has been derived from various sources. Please consult a licensed professional before attempting any techniques outlined in this book.

By reading this document, the reader agrees that under no circumstances is the author responsible for any losses, direct or indirect, which are incurred as a result of the use of the information contained within this document, including, but not limited to, — errors, omissions, or inaccuracies.

Introduction

"He who has never learned to obey cannot be a good commander" ~Aristotle

Life is much about learning, unlearning, and adapting to the waves of time.

There was a time, a few years ago, when business meetings translated to meetings in hotel lobbies, conference rooms, in the house of clients, or even approaching prospective clients on the streets. But one wave of time has washed it all away. Social media is the new hotspot for all our business meetings. You need to connect with all your clients online, and surely you need to make a lasting impression for it to work out. Online platforms of this day and age provide flexibility and help people gain authority over their communication skills, presentation, and more. Using online platforms to their best, can make us a virtual leader.

At present, virtual leadership skills are essential to make your business flourish. To become a Virtual leader, you first need a change of mindset. You need to bring in a fighter

Introduction

mentality—of someone who can sail through storms, in the middle of an ocean.

This is because with tough times come tough choices, unfathomable decisions, and twists of fate. Much like sailing a small boat in the wide ocean in the face of a storm.

Do you jump? Do you keep on sailing? Or do you throw your hands in the air and start wailing about why the world is so unfair?

Well, you can do any of these…but this choice of action will decide your fate.

For beyond this one storm, this one mammoth wave, is the rest of your path that you are yet to sail through to reach your goal.

If you give up now, you will never get to the other side. But if you brave through this storm instead, you will come out of it stronger.

Thus, this is a very important choice that you need to make. You, more than anyone else, because it is you who is rowing the boat. You are the ship's captain (or boat- up to your imagination), and your decision is key.

Storms in Real Life...

Now you may be thinking, why would you ever sail a boat in the middle of a storm? That's just too far-fetched for someone who spends most of their hours glued to the computer screen!

The storm is an analogy to get you thinking about the storms in real life. Of course, the storms in real life do not come with waves and winds but in the form of unforeseen obstacles to your dreams.

Introduction

All of us need to brave different storms on the way to success. You can't reach anywhere on a silent sea, can you?

But the thing is, the face of this storm varies for everyone. For example: while everyone around you seems to be sailing smoothly on the vast ocean of social networking, it seems nothing less than a giant wave crashing on your business, each time you try.

Maybe you have given up, at the sight of the storm, and maybe some people have jumped off to catch another. Maybe, more than the storm, you now feel lost in the vast ocean and scared that your boat may sink.

For someone who has sailed through their fair share of storms in life, let me tell you this: the only way ahead is through the eye of the storm. Forget those who jumped off your boat, they have never committed to the goal, anyway. Focus on leading those who remain, focus on braving this one storm with them, because after this, trust me, it gets better. To ensure it does get better for you, we are here.

Adapting to a Changing World

If you are still hesitant and feel that your current scenario can never flip for the better, here are some testimonials of real life people who made it through the storm.

At the age of 20, Sarah Robbins became the first network marketer and the youngest to be inducted into the Rodan + Fields Hall of Fame. Before network marketing, Sarah was a regular school teacher, earning a regular salary and living in the constant fear of going broke at any point. Sarah started selling products online in no time. She was earning six-figure commissions using a few targeted tips and tricks. This made it possible to quit her job, as a teacher, as she was now a millionaire network marketer.

This might make you feel that these success stories are only possible for youngsters, like Sarah. You are mistaken. There is a majority of middle-aged and even senior network marketers, who have made it big.

Donna Johnson, popularly known as the "Wisconsin girl with no college degree," was a single mom, of 5, when she started in network marketing. Starting brand new, in this field, was very challenging and to everyone's surprise she was successful. She now runs a team of multilevel marketers who earn approximately $45 – 50 million USD per month. If it was possible for Donna at her age, and situation, it is surely possible for you.

The Way of the Future

Wondering why all these success stories are linked solely to network marketing?

This is because network marketing is the only industry; that has boomed; after the onset of the pandemic. As most other industries, hospitality, took hard hits losing up to 94% of their customer base while network marketing flourished. Until 2019, the network marketing industry was around the $167 billion mark; in 2020, the pandemic happened, and it reached the $200 billion mark in that year itself. Very few industries saw such major growth.

But you may be thinking that the people who became millionaires, through network marketing, did so before the pandemic. Those examples do not seem very relevant now because no matter your age or qualifications, you are limited by this era of the remote-first, virtual-first system of

Introduction

marketing. So much seems to have changed so quickly that you are still trying to wrap your head around it. How would Donna or Sarah fare in the field of network marketing if they were to start today?

This is exactly why you need to revamp your knowledge of network marketing. Yes, Donna and Sarah had worked hard and used tips and tricks to ace their marketing skills, but those remain relevant in a different world: a world where people met face to face. Seems like a completely different era.

We have developed this ultimate guide to saving your sinking ship, using our years of experience in social networking and braving storms in real life.

No matter which stage you are stuck at trying to become a leader– at the end of this book, success awaits for all of you. You need to keep your hope alive and follow our guidelines, to sail through this storm.

Sailing Through the Storm Towards a Better Life...

For those of you who can't yet imagine the path after the storm, it's smoother, but not devoid of occasional storms. Keeping this in mind and building on our own experience, we have developed this book to guide you on becoming a leader everyone loves to follow despite the obstacles that may come your way.

The chapters of this book are planned and placed to make this a complete journey for everyone, even for someone who is hearing the term "network marketing" for the first time. All you need to do is follow our instructions and apply them to real-life settings.

Whether you are completely new to the world of

Introduction

network marketing or a leader, not where you want to be, we have you covered. If you're in the middle of the very first steps in network marketing, this book will help you overcome all the hurdles that are yet to come. With the challenge of building a team, finding the best social media platforms for engagement, or making your sales skyrocket, we will tackle every problem for you. Trust me, the process of overcoming these hurdles is more fun than you can imagine.

You will gain a refreshed insight into what it means to be a virtual leader in network marketing. Know which strategies work in a virtual setting and which strategies are ineffective from the old world. You will learn how to position yourself as an authority and set up your team for success.

You might be wondering why we sound so confident about this book we have written that supposedly claims to make you a leader. Is that even possible? Just by reading a book? If it were true, why aren't all librarians great leaders now? (no pun intended)

Well, puns apart, we understand your apprehensions, and we know where they come from. Believe it or not, we were once as confused and unsure as you are now. What changed that for us is learning, believing, and taking action. You can take the first steps in this process of change through this book, i.e., learning. Once you trust the strategies we provide in this book, you will surely develop confidence, a kind of confidence that only comes from knowledge. You can then utilize the knowledge and confidence through meaningful actions which are bound to make you a leader.

Good luck!

Introduction

Who are We?

We, Jose Sanchez and Irenne Rodriguez, have been network marketers for 15 years. We have built a global organization, the old way, and now, the new way.

Our organization continues to grow because we have applied the fundamentals of leadership, to our business. We aim to help the masses through this book, especially in this changing world where virtual interactions and screens have taken over. We know it can feel unsettling, you may be going through an identity crisis or losing confidence in your leadership abilities.

That is why we decided to write this book, using information and strategies relevant to today's world. Needless to say, these strategies were not developed in a day, nor were they easy. But, our hard work, decades of experience, and success make this book a great stepping stone for your journey in network marketing, in today's world.

Join Our Community on Facebook

To maximize the value you receive from this book, I highly encourage you to join our tight-knit community, on Facebook. Here you will be able to connect, learn and share strategies, to contain growth, as a network marketer. You can do so by scanning the QR code below with your camera phone. We look forward to connecting with you there.

Also by Jose Sanchez Macott and
Irenne Rodriguez

If you would like to learn how to get leads and prospects on social media, we recommend our book Social Media for Network Marketing Professionals: 9 Secret Steps Top Earners Use to Never Run Out of Prospects and Rank Advance in 90 days. To get the paperback copy or audiobook, simply scan the QR code below with your camera phone. This will take you directly to the amazon book's page. Enjoy!

Your Free Gift

As a way of saying thanks for your purchase, I'm offering a free guide that's exclusive to readers of the Leading Teams for Network Marketing Professionals book.

With the 9 Step Duplication Formula, for Network Marketing, you will discover a printable reference guide that will help you duplicate your team and income. It will help your network marketing business to the next level.

Grab the guide by scanning the QR code below with your camera phone or go to **www.sanchezmacott.com**

1

What is a Great Virtual Leader in Network Marketing?

So, you have turned to the first chapter of this book to start building or maybe rebuilding your career in network marketing. And you know you don't want to be one among the millions of network marketers who are happy in their limited niche. You want to become a network marketing leader, a virtual leader who can make a mark in this field.

You may think that leaders are born and not made. Your mind traces back to John, that one student in your class who seemed to have natural leadership skills. Whatever he did, people always looked up to him and tended to listen to him. That's what a leader is, isn't it?

Let me tell you, leaders like John are not born with it. Your peer, John, must have worked in the right direction to shape himself as a leader. Or maybe John had clear answers to the questions that set you up on the path to becoming a leader: who do I want to become? What level of success do I want to reach? Do I want to lead or be led? Finding answers to these questions can be a tricky road, which I am sure you all have dealt with already, and it has led you here.

If not, you can ask yourself these questions. It will help you define your goal set. Having a definite set of goals before diving into this chapter will make all my secret strategies more effective.

So, we understand that the skills of becoming a network marketing leader, need not be a natural talent. You can acquire them with practice. But everyone needs a starting point, right? You need to know whether you are right at the starting line with others, ready to sprint on the track as the whistle blows, or you still have a few miles to go before running.

This book will work for everyone looking to become a leader in network marketing, but how fast and effective it will work will depend on where you stand now.

Think of what you have. Determination? Hardwork? Motivation? Discipline? Routine? If you have any of these, it's a great beginning. If you don't have any of these, it's still a great beginning.

4 Steps to Shape Yourself into a Leader

Step 1: Internal Mastery

No, it's not just the monks who need it. And this certainly doesn't require hours of meditation (although meditation is a healthy practice to keep up).

Remember the story of braving storms in real life? Here is the first storm you must brave: the one inside your head. The storms that mess with your head. It varies for different people. For some, inconsistencies in the market can mess with their focus, or for some, a sloppy team gets them frustrated. You may also suffer from confidence issues, nervousness while communicating with others, and more. All these are indicators of Self-doubt, which is the biggest storm you must brave to become a leader.

The only way to emerge steady on the other side of this storm, is by working on your personal development. For a while, forget about everything else. Forget how much commission Mary made last month and how Jack is moving into his new penthouse. Forget all of it.

Focus on yourself. Train your mind every day. Learn the art of restraint and control. Learn to steady the storms, inside your head.

If you are unwilling to work on yourself, believe in your skills and back yourself up. No one will.

The one reason leaders can effectively lead, is because they have already led themselves through multiple storms. They know that storms are common, obstacles are waiting for them, and they are ready to face and overcome them. If you have this confidence that you can pull yourself through, this confidence will echo in your team. And leading them won't be as difficult, as it is now.

But how do you know that you're going to pull through? Because at this day and time, while you have this book in your hand, you don't know for sure that you will pull through.

Well, this knowledge comes from confidence, and this confidence comes from knowledge.

"Knowledge is power" this quote is as old as time, propagated by Sir Francis Bacon in 1597!

And centuries later, it has not ceased to be true.

You need to live by this quote to begin shaping your "leadership mindset." Your level of knowledge will distinguish you from others and help you reach the finish line before anyone else.

Here are the Three Levels of Knowledge-Based Self-Development:

Level 1: Develop Knowledge About Your Field

This is where most people get eliminated, from becoming a leader. Trust me, only 1% of people, with leadership dreams, reach this level of knowledge. Once you are in this league, there is no looking back. It just gets better and better.

Reaching this 1% is a task that requires consistency, investment of time, and focus. But the returns of this investment are very, very high (which I will come to, soon).

We are who we are based on what we read, listen to, and surround ourselves with. Your immediate environment has obvious effects on your mind.

For example, if you keep a plant on a dark shelf, without the essential sunlight, and you don't water it– that plant will never bear fruit and wither before you know it. To keep it alive and see the fruits come to life, you have to water it every day! You are not very different from that plant. Your brain needs the daily dose of water (knowledge from reading) to keep you on this path to becoming a successful leader.

So, when I talk about reading, it is crucial to read as much as you can possibly find on everything relevant to network marketing. Here is a checklist of books you can begin with (to amplify your learnings from this book) in the field of network marketing-

- As a Man Thinketh - James Allen

- What to Say When You Talk to Yourself - Shad Helmstetter
- Freakishly Effective Leadership for Network Marketers- Ray Higdon
- Magic of Thinking Big - David J. Schwartz
- Unemployed Millionaire- Matt Morris
- Social Media for Network Marketing Professionals by Jose Sanchez Macott and Irenne Rodriguez

Six books. That's what it takes to be in the 1% league of topmost, knowledgeable network marketers. If you clear this threshold, you will leave most wannabe network marketing leaders behind. Why? Because most people are too lazy to read six books on the same topic. Thus, if you do it, you become more knowledgeable and an expert in the field by default.

Level 2: Develop Your Willpower

Your willpower can drive you through the worst storms in life, pick you up from the most hopeless ruts and set you up for success. No, I am not referring to the kind of willpower that comes and goes with each morning alarm. I am talking about the willpower that ignites your actions and boosts your consistency. And this willpower comes from your mind. You have to get into an "I will execute it, I will get the results, I will make it happen" mindset. On your good days, and most importantly, on your bad days. Holding on to your willpower on your bad days is what solidifies it. This willpower will often take the driver's seat in your life when all else: your skills, your luck, and your experiences, fail you.

If you need to practice manifestations to develop your

willpower, do it every day. If you need visual stimulations-use motivational quote posters in your room, and watch Ted Ex videos. Do as much as you can to keep up your willpower every day.

Level 3: Develop Confidence

Your knowledge and willpower can make you a fighter and help you achieve internal mastery. But, it's your self-confidence that makes you a leader. Because people can sense it, they can sense your self-doubt and self-confidence. While the first will scare them off, the second will make them believe you, as a leader. Self-confidence is of the utmost importance, in becoming a virtual leader: because it shows you know what you're talking about. You know how this field works. You know how to master this field. How do you know? You know, because you read those six books on the same topic that others didn't. You know because you watered your mind every day. You know because you have a stable (and not flaky) willpower, to make things work.

Your self-confidence is the ultimate fruit that your efforts of internal mastery will bear. Master your mind and then project that mastery to the outer world. Before leading others, you have to ace self-leadership. "Discipline your discipline" every day, and with enough practice, you will become the natural leader that you thought John was.

Not everyone reaches this level, many have given up, due to lack of internal mastery. Leaders have to control their emotions: getting mad, angry, or frustrated will mess with your mind. This makes people give up. Business is difficult on the inside, not on the outside. Skills can be gained. Skills can be taught. Skills can be honed. But internal mastery cannot. Massive success and staying successful takes internal mastery. A lot of external things will try to knock you of your path. But having your internal zen will help you brave through storms.

Step 2: External Mastery

Once you have mastered your mind, you are ready to start the next quest: external mastery.

Meaning the mastery of skills that a network marketing leader needs. In general, in any field, a leader has both: internal and external mastery.

Let's say you have finished those six books and now you are equipped with a lot of knowledge. Now, what do you do with that knowledge? You grow it, and as you grow it, you keep executing it.

Execute the strategies, tactics, and tips in your real-life scenario daily.

If you have devoured six books on effective communication, try some of the tips you've learned when talking to prospects or people from your team.

Keep a note of what worked for you and what didn't. Read more on the topic to improve the areas that didn't work for you or find better-suited tactics for your situation. Read six more books on effective communication, try those in your next meeting, keep a note of what worked and what didn't, and keep repeating this until you are sure that you can get through every stage of effective communication.

Now do the same for every essential skill in your field of work. If you're a network marketer, work on your marketing knowledge, communication, presentation skills, persuasion skills, social media skills, content creation skills, and so on.

And if you want to be a successful virtual leader, let me tell you, these skills must be applied all the time.

There won't come the point where you know too much or everything about network marketing.

Having knowledge only, without practice, will not lead you anywhere.

Shake off the laziness and get excited. Not being lazy is what will distinguish you. If you want to level up, read 30 books and become unbeatable. If you expect and dream this field to earn you million-dollar profits and thrive in your business, and not just be any other Jack and Sally who is a network marketer, you have to outdo yourself and challenge yourself to become the top 1% of that 1% and so on. Those who are too lazy to apply these skills will automatically fall behind you. So make a profit off of other people's laziness. Become a unique source of knowledge on network marketing and people will start to look up to you and think of you when they think of network marketing.

To make sure that you are on the right path and you are indeed effectively executing the knowledge you have gathered, you can simply practice these 4 steps-

·**Challenge Yourself**

Face those challenges head-on. Use your willpower and back it up with your knowledge to get through the challenges. If a presentation needs to be made in a week, volunteer for it. Take on the challenge, and then try to sail through it the best you can. If there is a meeting you need to handle, don't shy away from it. Execute the tips that you have learned and repeat the trial and error process.

·**Try and Fail**

Exposing yourself means that you are trying to deal with the challenges. Trying also means that there is a 50% chance of failing. So try and fail. Maybe in 10 attempts of using the acquired skills, you will win 3 times and fail the other 7. That is okay, as long as you readily accept challenges and practice what you have learned.

·Fail Again

It may happen that you don't even have 3 wins in your 10 attempts. Maybe all of your attempts are failing, and it's starting to vigorously rattle your inner peace. Don't let it. Tell yourself that failing is equivalent to succeeding in this journey. Failing means you tried, and you win as long as you try.

·Move Beyond the Fear of Failing

There aren't any entrepreneurs who haven't failed.

The multi-millionaire owner of IBM once said- "if you want to greatly increase the success in your life, double the rate of failure." This is because the more you deal with failures, the more fearless you become. Your first failure may seem like a huge setback to you, the second won't as much, neither will the third…and somewhere down the line, failure's value will diminish in your journey. Your fear of failure will be long gone, and this will give you the confidence to try, even if you fail.

To sum it up, your success in external mastery depends on how often you execute the knowledge you have learned, not how well you execute it. It also matters how you deal with your failures and fear of facing challenges. The more you try, the more you fail and the more fearless you become. You see, this is what keeps the ball rolling and helps you gain momentum in this journey.

Step 3: Focus on Your Relationships and Influence

Your success as a network marketing leader in this virtual world relies 80% on your relationship with your team. No, I am not talking about developing personal relationships here, I mean how you deal with your team members. In what tone do you talk to them? Are you empathetic towards them? Do you show that you value them? Do you believe in them so that they believe in themselves too?

These are soft skills that no one ever focuses on. The majority of people will say in their pitch that they are focused, hardworking and diligent, and thus, they can be good leaders. Sorry, in the real world, that doesn't cut it. Your hard work is your own. Your diligence is your virtue. It doesn't directly translate to people. This doesn't influence your team. Your hard work is in your interest. You need to show that you have your team's or client's best interests at heart, well and above your own!

Otherwise, as a network marketer, how will you ever sell the same things over and over again, to the same people, online?

At this stage in your journey, you are knowledgeable and have the essential skills of a network marketer, but the effects of these are limited to you.

How will your team and your clients gain from this?

You must build a bridge between your qualities and your team's needs. This bridge is no less than a trustworthy relationship, a solid friendship between you and your peers.

Now, this might have been possible when you met people in person, talked to them with direct eye contact, and understood their body language.

Building this bridge of trust with online interactions is tough. I completely acknowledge that.

But, it is not impossible.

Here are a few tips that can help you develop your influence during virtual interactions:

·Be Completely Present and Listen Well

If you take advantage of the mute button on Zoom and do stuff you shouldn't do during meeting, then it is a clear sign of how disinterested you are in the meeting. And this sign is completely clear to those on the other side of the screen the moment you mute yourself and turn off your camera. You have to show with your actions that you're not interested in only the bits and parts of the meeting, but you are completely present during the meeting and are actively listening. A good way is to take notes during the meeting and provide feedback (relevant feedback, wherever necessary).

·Have a Positive Energy

Don't think that screens don't give off vibes. They sure do. Your body language is the main carrier of your energy. If you intend to have a positive vibe during your meeting, make sure your body language matches it. Do not sit in a way that is off or look elsewhere on the screen when you're talking to someone. In the end, these are the little things that sum up as a whole to determine your influence on people. You can follow some of these tips before your next virtual meeting.

·Dress for a Real-Life Meeting

I know that the real perk of working online is not having to get ready for the "office", but, for network marketers, their desk at home is their office. There is no way that you should be informal, casual clothes during virtual meetings. How seriously you dress up for the meeting equates to how seriously you take your client.

You don't wanna be messing that up!

Let people know you believe in them!

No matter the idea, no matter the plans that are coming off from the other side of the screen, let people know that you believe in their vision. That you believe in them. Leaders are much needed in this world because people need someone to validate their beliefs. What people want is to believe in themselves and be confident. That's exactly what people fail to do without a leader. As a leader, if you believe in your team, your team will believe in you. This is how exactly why they will follow your lead.

· **Follow-up**

Don't forget the meetings once they are over. Don't wait 10 days to get back to your customers when you promised you'd get in touch in a day. In conclusion, don't be unorganized in your communications. Follow up after the meetings, check the progress, and answer any queries seriously and timely. If required, schedule your emails, beforehand, to ensure you're at the top of your game.

You need to effectively blend in these soft skills with your knowledge and willpower, to make a difference.

Step 4: Find your Strengths and Focus on your Weaknesses

This is a secret tip that many do not know. Usually, most personal development books will tell you to find your strengths, focus on them, and hone them to become a leader.

Your strengths and inherent qualities make up an important part of your leadership skills, but your focus should first be on your weaknesses.

Think of this scenario, you are trying to drive a bicycle from point A to point B, which is 5 miles away, but the road is filled with tree branches and debris from a previous storm.

If you try to ride your bicycle through this, it will be tricky. The ride will surely be difficult with so many obstacles in your way, and cycling through it will frustrate you and might even make you want to give up!

An effective way, through this will be to remove all the branches from the road and then have a smooth ride to the finish line.

Similarly, in the journey to becoming a leader, they will keep pulling you back if you don't focus on your weaknesses will keep pulling you back, if you ignore them. They will pile up and hinder your progress.

So, before you hone your strengths, identify your weaknesses, and work on them.

If you know your communication skills are lacking, read more than five books on it. Practice your speech and body language in front of a mirror.

If you need to work on your persuasion skills more, read more books on psychology, how to influence people, and execute the strategies, as you go.

In the meanwhile, take your strengths along with you. Your strengths will give you a basic level of confidence as you start and help you gain momentum, but improving your weaknesses will be a breakthrough.

If you are not yet sure what your skill set is, at the moment and what your strengths and weaknesses are, try this quick exercise below.

Quick Brain Exercise:

Practice:
  · List all of your skills on a paper
  · Rate your skills on a scale of 1-10 (1 being weak to 10 being strength)

- Rate each skill as a strength or a weakness based on this score.

Prioritize working on the skills with a score below 5 first, and then gradually work your way upwards. This will help you develop the ultimate leadership skill set you need for success.

These are the four building pillars of a leader: internal mastery, external mastery, relationships, influencing skills, and knowing your weaknesses and strengths. This will get you started in the right direction to becoming a successful virtual leader.

But what do you think a good virtual leader is made of?

5 Qualities of a Good Network Marketing Leader

1. Confident

They say, "first impression is very important". Well, I think every impression is just as important. Every virtual meeting is a chance to make or break your image. Being confident: the right amount of confidence, not overconfident and cocky and certainly not underconfident and meek, is the balance you need to find. A good virtual leader sets themselves apart from the crowd with their confidence quotient. You can spot a leader in a mass of hundreds just by the way they speak or carry themselves.

2. Capable

A good virtual leader is certainly an expert in their field. Their knowledge levels in their area of work are always very advanced and they do not stop acquiring knowledge. They constantly upgrade themselves. This is what makes a leader, successfully in their position.

3. Committed

A good virtual leader is committed to themselves first; their ideas and cause; and their team; and then their clients. A good virtual leader also knows how to value commitments; meeting targets, or being on time for a meeting. Commitment is an abstract virtue, but in leaders, their actions clearly express the commitment to their work daily.

4. Coachable

A good leader is willing to learn from others. Someone with strict foundations and a narrow niche is far away from becoming a leader. A leader is coachable, willing to learn, adapt to the times, and modify their ways to meet certain requirements. A bendable stick will never break. A flexible leader will adapt to the circumstances.

5. Good Communicator

This is a given skill that any good leader must have. Communication is key. It's only with effective communication that you can influence people and lead them, or even build bridges, with your clients. Average communication skills will not be effective. A good virtual leader is someone who has sharpened their communication skills perfectly. When they speak, you will keep thinking that they are born with this skill, but they have learned and through hard work have mastered this skill.

What's Holding You Back from Becoming a Virtual Leader?

So now that you have gathered knowledge about how successful leaders are made and how to recognize one, you must be asking yourself, why aren't you one?

Here are the 4 possible answers to your question-

·**Fear and Overwhelm**

You are uncertain of what to do and don't know where to start. If this is the case, this chapter can very well provide the foundation for your goal of becoming a virtual leader. Ask yourself why and how you would like to become one. Until and unless you define your why's and hows, you will keep feeling lost. You need to eliminate your overwhelm by creating a plan for self-improvement as you start this journey.

·Passive Action

Educating but not putting the action. This is a stage where most people give up. They start to get motivated and buy all the books they need, but after reading 2 books in a row, they wonder how it is even helping them. And they give up. This is because they didn't execute their learnings, in real life. You need to utilize the concepts and strategies daily to make any active progress.

·Becoming Responsible for Your Thoughts

Always think of good outcomes, not bad. This is a mindset that will surely fail you. Yes, reading this book or working on your self-development is a great way to start, but the outcomes won't always be positive. Instead, you need to see the world in more than black and white. You need to ground yourself in reality and accept that there will be gray days where you fail. You need to analize what went wrong, what went right and act accordingly.

·Understand the Importance of Taking Action

Yes builds the business, nos will strengthen your drive to build a successful business. This is the most important piece of advice that I can give you. After each rejection and after each failure, you need to take action and fix things up for better the next time. The rejections and nos will build up a fighting mentality, ultimately building your business.

Tips

- To be hugely successful in any field, you have to be an expert in that field.
- You need to take action and execute your knowledge
- You have to fail and then move beyond failing
- You need to focus on your weaknesses before your strengths.

Let's say you have successfully mastered your leader mindset and have gathered great deal of knowledge on network marketing. Now, what do you do with this knowledge? How do you channel it into starting your business? We have gathered realistic strategies for this based on decades of our own experiences. The next chapter will advice you how to transform this knowledge into a business plan that people will engage with.

2

Position Yourself as an Authority

The last chapter was to help you understand that becoming a virtual leader requires a certain mindset. It also needs internal and external mastery before you start seeing results. But if you plan on waiting until you have satisfactorily achieved internal and external mastery, take this next step.

All these chapters are intended to be a comprehensive guide to becoming a network marketing leader, and you'll have to try out two to three things in tandem to make progress.

Becoming an authority, a.k.a leader in your field (no matter your field), has much to do with your multitasking skills. So, as you grab your first or second book on network marketing in your internal mastery journey, you'll also have to grab your guiding light (this book) and apply the strategies given in this chapter.

You now know all the qualities that make a great virtual leader, from the knowledge to the body language you need. But how do you channel that to other people? Through communication! But how do you communicate the overwhelming amount of knowledge you keep gathering (considering you're taking your internal mastery journey seriously)? And why would people even listen to you when you struggle with the first steps?

It is possible. It's possible to communicate your knowledge (no matter how much you have gained), and it's possible to position yourself as an authority, even if you're just getting started!

This chapter is to help you take your first step in implementing what you have learned, so far, or are learning at the moment. To sail through the storm, you must first drive yourself straight into it! Consider these steps much like that. How unphased and fast you get out of the storm is determined by how determined and consistent you are to get to the other side.

Where to Begin?

Positioning yourself as an authority is not an overnight game; it takes a little while and depends on your consistency. If you give up after taking a single step, it won't work out.

This is the most crucial stage: getting started. If you get into motion, you'll most likely stay in that motion (some real-life physics scenario), but that comes later.

Right now, you need to get out of your shell! You can say you don't have one, and you're a social person who likes interacting with others. Okay, that can be a good starting point, but there is a difference between chatting with your friends and speaking from a leader's point of view.

If you're shy and have social anxiety, you will need to work a little harder. Nonetheless, it's possible.

Once you're sure where you stand and how comfortable you are in interacting with others, you need to upgrade your presence and body language as you interact. You can refer to the first chapter again to get this done.

Next, becoming curious and asking questions or getting involved in conversations. If you see a group of your teammates randomly discussing stuff related to a work topic, jump in. Resist the urge to leave the room because you're scared you'll say something stupid. During meetings with your team, get curious, and ask questions. At any point in time, a million thoughts run through an average person's mind. Ask away, and if you don't get your answer, research it on your own time.

Who knows, maybe your teammate had a similar experience but was scared to bring it forward. Now that you have done your research, you can start a conversation with your teammate about it!

There, you have just taken the first step out of your shell. Try to be more interactive and inquisitive, daily. Speak up when you have the urge to, it might be uncomfortable at first, but gradually it will become second nature. Your immediate environment, like team meetings, is great to get started.

The outcome is that people in your team will start seeing you as someone who takes the lead, let that be in random conversations or meetings. Once you start sharing your experience with your teammates, they will recognize how invested you are in your field. No matter how much passion you have in your heart, it is as good as nothing if you don't show what you know.

Remember...

Be cautious not to overdo it. There is a line of balance between being a leader and behaving like one. Don't just make statements and start conversations for the sake of it. Speak with substance, that can only be done if you're gathering knowledge and working on your internal mastery. Just as I said, you need to do things in tandem.

But, Can You Be an Expert if You're Not an Expert?

I am sure a part of your mind is telling you that the previous advice will not work! Why would people listen to you or see you as a leader if all of you are at the same professional level? Why would you be considered a leader?

Well, first, you're reading those 6 books, per topic, that others aren't. This automatically upgrades your position, in the team, in terms of knowledge.

Second, as you interact and talk about your passion and your journey in network marketing: your aims; how you set up your goals; and what you're reading at the moment; it immediately resonates with people who want to do the same but aren't doing so at the moment. This is how you can become a symbol of inspiration for others.

Think about this for a moment– what do you do when you feel that you are not fit and need to change your diet and get moving? You Google "how to get fit in 10 days," then Google guides you to the most viewed and liked videos on Youtube about getting fit in 10 days. But there is a twist to this- to you, who is a beginner, the videos of advanced trainers who workout like a total pro won't work as well as watching the journey of someone who was once like you and then pushed themselves to get fit in 10 days. I can guarantee that the second video is what you would opt for. This is because it's closer to reality, your reality, and thus it impacts you more.

You need to become that person on the other end of the screen who is on a journey and sharing their journey with others. It doesn't matter if you are just beginning because they will witness seeing your progress and become better.

This is how you gain a position of authority— you make the journey, you do the trials and errors, and then people learn from you.

It doesn't matter if you are learning. People can learn from your mistakes too. So, it's absolutely a myth that you can't become an expert or take up a leading role until you're an expert, yourself. For the first few months of your journey of becoming a virtual leader, you are already in a leading position as you're in the field. You're taking action and trying every day. At the same time, those watching you are learning from you and watching you.

You must share as you learn that you expose yourself to the world. Your journey to becoming a virtual leader can become someone's inspiration. When you begin sharing your journey, you claim your position of authority!

Get the Ball Rolling...

So, exactly do you share your journey with others?

There can be as many ways as you'd like. If you're comfortable in front of the camera, you can create your YouTube channel. If you don't have the time to make full-fledged videos, make reels or shorts. Quick but effective video tips can be very engaging. You can share your videos on social media to help them reach more people and create engagement.

If you're camera shy and would rather not get into the hassle of video editing and posting- you can write blogs. Multiple blogging sites are free to use and work amazingly, like WordPress or Medium. Get out there and post on your blog every day. Check the engagement and traffic on your blog site and find ways to enhance it. You can similarly share and tweet your blogs to help them reach a larger audience.

Regardless of which one you choose, make sure it's visually pleasing. With the videos and reels, it's a given. But if you decide to blog about your journey, keep each post very visual and limit using large chunks of text. This quickly makes it very boring, and your audience may move on from your post.

The key to creating content is to include visually attractive elements like pictures, motivating captions, or catchy headlines to get viewers and readers hooked. Otherwise, why would anyone spend their precious time learning about your journey, with millions of other posts on the web?

Remember...

When I say make it visually pleasing, I don't mean doing an art project. Carry out some research, find out what's in trend. Watch videos of other top earners and what content they are using and see how they are doing theirs. Don't copy that exactly, that's never going to work. But learn from their way of doing things and incorporate your ideas into it. This is to ensure that you're relevant in the media and that you're not doing anything bizarre that doesn't influence people the way you want to.

If you're scratching your head thinking, what in the world can you get started with? Here's an easy checklist of headlines that you can use for your first video or blog.

Fill in the gaps based on the topic of your choice and leave the rest up to me-

Headline for your first post (Stevens, 2017)

- 3 Ways You Can Quickly _____
- Discover How to _____
- Do You Make These _____ Mistakes?
- Do You Make These Mistakes in _____?
- Here's How to End Your _____ Problems For Good... And Use This Surprisingly Simple _____ to _____ FAST
- You're About to Discover How to _____ and _____
- How to _____ and _____
- What's the Best Way To _____?
- Who Else Want to Discover _____ Secrets of the World's Top/Best _____?
- Stop _____ and Discover a Simple _____

This is an exclusive collection of headlines that I had especially curated for my journey, and I can guarantee you, that these work!

Don't Market Stuff, Market Information

It's crucial to understand what you're saying and why you're saying it. Well, it's true for all moments in life, but more so when you're sharing your insights on network marketing, on the web. Whether it's a blog, a video, or a social media post, you need to have a defined goal for each.

Every other person in the United States will try to sell you some product. They can be very good at convincing people, but they still can fail.

Most people lose interest in your content, when they realize you're trying to sell a product, because they won't gain anything from it. Well, they get the product, but they get it in exchange for an investment. They need to invest their hard-earned money. That is not something everyone is keen to do, solely based on 5 minutes of convincing talk. Most people will skip the video or scroll to another blog post because buying some product is not in their interest.

What people are interested in is solutions. Quick and easy solutions can work for them with minimal effort and time. Everyone is busy. No one will spend 5 minutes listening to your journey if you're not imparting any useful knowledge.

People may not buy stuff all the time, but they always, always buy information (Cummings, 2022). And that is exactly what your videos or blogs should be based on. Information on how you got started on your journey, information on what you read to gain knowledge on network marketing, information on things you have tried out in this field, things that worked, and even things that failed!

As long as you provide useful information that helps

people move ahead in their journey in exchange for their time, your posts will never go out of trend!

The best thing about this is information will never go out of date. No matter how many years down the line, someone will always be willing to start on their journey, feeling lost or wanting to restart their network marketing career. All of these people can rely on your content to get started. This is how, even as a beginner, you can lead people and gain a position of authority.

Attraction Marketing...and Why it Works!

You can make a mark in network marketing by attracting people on social media using your real-life experiences and communication skills. This strategy is also known as attraction marketing. Use social media, as a tool in your journey, to becoming a leader.

You could make a video on that itself- "how to harness the power of social media for your business?" See! Nothing you do in this journey will go to waste, from your wins to your failures. Everything is useful to someone out there!

People get hooked on real-life experiences and solutions to real-life problems- it helps them connect to you. By telling people all about your experiences, struggles, and solutions to your network marketing journey, you will become a trustable resource. When they face similar problems in their journey, they will look up your solutions and information.

The more consistently you share information, the more people will follow your content. This sets a positive cycle in motion: with a rising number of followers, you will also feel responsible towards them and keep creating content for them, the more you create, the better you are in the field of network marketing. And this goes on and on to make you an unparalleled leader.

As you advance in your journey in network marketing, you can talk about advanced problems and solutions, but you also have content for beginners that you created when you first started. This will make your social platform a one-stop information site for all the information and tips they need. It is extremely important to make content, when becoming a successful leader.

This whole positive cycle of attraction marketing will build you a strong base for becoming a virtual leader. The sooner you start on this journey, the better your results will be.

How to Keep the Ball Rolling...?

Somewhere down the line, you will ask yourself this question- "how do I keep the ball rolling"? "How do I hold on to the position of authority, long after I have gained it?"

This is an important question, and I have a credible answer for this.

To ensure that your content, information, and your position of authority don't become a thing of the past, you need to be consistent about the following things:

Find Your Niche

Make sure you know what you want to talk about. Yes, this is important for each video/blog along the way. But this is also important as a whole. You need to find a topic that you know a lot about and are comfortable with and want to invest your time daily. So, if you're aiming to become a network marketing leader, and one day you think of talking about your fitness journey instead- it can be a hit or miss. In my experience, it will mostly be a miss. Stick to your goal and keep it consistent.

Focus on a Single Thing for Each Video or Blog Post

I cannot stress how important this is. I have seen many virtual leaders provide information in bits and pieces about multiple things scattered in a video. As a viewer, your mind will be confused about the main takeaways! And do you think a confused viewer will tune in to your videos a second time? NO.

Be Sure About Your Target Audience and Curate Your Content Keeping Their Needs in Mind

This is as important as finding your niche. Be sure who you are reaching to. Whom do you want to become a leader for? What would you be curious about? This will help you streamline your video/blog content and organize it in a relatable manner.

Find a Style

Every leading content creator has a style. Maybe their style in 2 informative 2-minute videos or videos that provide quick and easy tips at the end. Brainstorm on this, and add a unique element to your content that sets you apart from the network marketing vloggers/bloggers pool.

Product or Business Opportunity, What Should Lead the Way?

While trying to expand your business online and focusing on getting leads, you need to be cautious about what you're leading with. Are you focusing on providing a business opportunity to your audience? Or you're trying to promote the benefits of your product and trying to make sales? Your content should be in tune with your leading aspect. We recommend you use a balanced proportion of both- product promotion and business opportunity in your content. Your audience will be a mix of people who like the product and network marketing, enthusiasts. Thus, when you're curating your video or blog content, you need to keep it interesting for both these groups (C., 2021). This will ensure that you're not missing out on prospective enrollees while you're busy making sales. Balance is key!

However, it's important to remember that it is okay, no matter what your leading with, even if you lose the balance from time to time. As long as you're sharing your knowledge, connecting, and helping your online community, you are someone they will surely look up to.

Takeaway:

- Teach as you learn, and learn as you teach. As you start implementing what you're learning about network marketing, this should be your mantra.
- Expose yourself to the world, share your ideas, information, struggles, and tips on making it as a network marketer. Everyone loves free and useful information.
- Be consistent in sharing your journey. This will create a positive cycle of getting more leads and increasing the number of people who look up to you.

Once you apply these strategies and start gaining enrollees for your business, you will also have to guide them in the right direction so that they enjoy network marketing while working for your business. Now, this is no easy task and puts even the best leaders to test. To know how to effectively engage your enrollees in your business, turn the page to the next chapter.

3

Launch New Enrollees to the Moon

So, you have successfully marketed your stuff, exposed yourself to the world, and people have started listening to you. They are excited and want to go all the way in your business. You feel like you have cracked the deal already! You have a boat full of people ready to follow you into the storm. But you want them to row your boat for you, take care of the radar, direction, and much more. And before you know it, their motivation is out of the window, and they want to jump off the boat and move on to a better boat.

Gradually, it sinks into you that you're now back to square one! You have to begin again! You have to again search for new prospects and find other people to close (to enroll in your business). And you go on and on in this loop, but no one sticks around.

But why does this happen? Why would the same people, whose eagerness was bursting through the screen just two days ago, vanish like that? Without a word?

You may think that these particular enrollees didn't have it in them, maybe their motivation was superficial, or they weren't committed enough. So you try again, but again, the same result. And this keeps happening.

Before you begin another loop of the same process, pause— and assess your approach toward your new enrollees. Maybe it was you and not them. Maybe they were lost and didn't receive the training, they had hoped for. This may have killed their motivation to get into network marketing. Now, if you go ahead with your previous approach, there is a strong chance that the results will also be the same as before.

But how do you move forward without winning this phase? Without building a team?

You need to follow the strategies in this chapter to a T, and you won't have to worry about losing enrollees anymore!

Let's start with what you shouldn't do, once people have signed up for your business, and then we will go over all the things you should do, to launch them to the moon!

First Things First, Don't Scare Your Enrollees Away...

What to avoid with your new connections?

If you're doing any of the things below with your new enrollees, it is your problem, not theirs. Go over the scenarios and see how many you can relate with. Remember, be honest with yourself.

- **You talk to them about targets on the first day**

Imagine you are someone who has finally made a move, to sign up for a network marketing business, after days of debating about it. A successful network marketing business would help you improve your living conditions or pay off your debts. You join in hopes of learning, gaining skills and making money.

The person you have put your trust in is someone you have been following, on social media, and you think they are amazing and so knowledgeable. The first day, you are given targets to fulfill and it is daunting. You don't know how to do any of them, if you knew, you would have started a network marketing business!

So imagine how horrified your new enrollee will get if you hand them a list of targets, on their first day when they know nothing about how things work. You may think what did they learn, from your videos, all these days, then? Well, those videos were you talking about your experiences. For them to have some experience in the first place, they need to know where to begin! So, consider this before hitting your enrollee with targets to fulfill on the first day. (Simone, 2020).

- **You ask them for results in the first five days**

Now, you may have reached that part of your journey, where you want to start earning profits and expanding your business. That is why you want to get more people involved in your business.

Imagine your enrollees trying to get results in 5 days, which took you months to get! Isn't that an unrealistic expectation from someone who has just begun? Don't ask them for results, immediately. Give them space to try and fail, if needed. This will help them realize that you're with them, on this.

- **You give them a long list of prospects to close**

Okay, results and targets aside, can't the new enrollees, at least, call a list of prospects and get the ball rolling? You may think so! Imagine a very introverted person or someone with social anxiety, having to do this on their first day! Could it get any worse? So, this is also something you should avoid, pushing your enrollees on the first day.

- **You tell them to engage and make social media content for the business**

This can be even more difficult, than calling up random people, not everyone is tech-savvy and a social media person. You can have retired people, in your team, who have never used a smartphone, let alone Instagram. You need to be ready to accept this and find ways to help them get started.

- **You want them to show you numbers- of people, profits, and more!**

You may think, isn't that what business owners do? Ask their team members to work and get profits. Well, network marketing is not a stereotypical business. It relies on building loyal relationships with prospects and your team. Thus, ask your enrollees to focus on getting acquainted with contacting people and making new relationships first, and then aim for people and profits!

Remember, people may be ready to follow your lead, at first, and have a lot of enthusiasm, but, it's your job to utilize that enthusiasm and keep it intact throughout the stormy journey! We all know network marketing is not an easy-breezy, money-making strategy. You need to put in work and go through a lot of ups and downs, before you hit the jackpot. So, your people should be ready to take that journey with you. If you wear out their enthusiasm by drowning them in work, as soon as they start, no one will stick.

What to Do to Launch Your Enrollees into Network Marketing

1. Direct your enrollees to the correct path

You need to do for your enrollees what this book is doing for you: guide. You need to remember that they are beginners, they don't know the A-B-C of network marketing, and you are their leader, guide and boss, all in one!

Yes, it is a demanding job, but you can do this easily because you have trained yourself, too!

Remember! You need to lead yourself first before you can lead others!

Now is the time to get into action.

Remind them of the important things and core values, of network marketing, that they should always remember:

- **Their story:** They need to be clear about their story related to the product. What got them interested in this business, in the first place? Why do they want to be a part of it? How does this add meaning to their life? All of this adds to their personal story, about this business, which can be shared with their prospects, to create a bond! Ask them to define their story, before they start.

- **Why do they believe in the product?** This is part of their story and the most integral part. How did this product help them? Why do they want to let others know about this product? How do they think it can help others? Your new enrollees need to have the answers to these questions figured out when they start. This will help them be more confident when talking to people as they start networking.
- **What's their goal?** Essentially, what do they want to achieve, as part of your business? Is it a career shift? Is it their first time doing a business, on their own? Do they want to increase their confidence and social presence? There can be as many reasons as there are people. As long as, they are clear on this, their mindset will be strong.
- **How can they earn their money back with profits?** This is something that all the enrollees will undoubtedly wonder about! This can be the major motivation for most of them too. But you need to help them believe it's possible, they just need to trust you and retain the same enthusiasm. If you don't provide the reassurance, there's a big chance they will drop out of the business.

So, no matter how many enrollees you get in a day, you must follow these rules with each and everyone of them, to make sure they stick with you, in this journey.

2. Train your enrollees in the basics!

People from all sorts of backgrounds get into network marketing, it can be their sole source of income or a side hustle. You should have the tools to guide and train everyone. The chance that someone ,with network marketing skills, will enroll in your business, is unlikely. Be ready to have enrollees who have not had any exposure to social media, let alone, network marketing.

They might have just joined because they believe in your ideology. Maybe they don't even know what network marketing is. Based on my experience in this field, I must say, that most network marketers don't have high-level skills, such as those obtained through a college education or professional experience.

Be ready to train highly motivated people with limited skills. So, how do you train this group of enrollees successfully? Follow these steps (Higdon, 2021)

- **Don't use jargon:** Jargons are essentially technical terms. Your enrollees don't know what "prospecting" or "auto-ship" means. I mean, these are the terms you learned after reading multiple books on network marketing. So, this knowledge is specific to you. You must avoid using technical terms with your enrollees, in the first few weeks of joining. Using jargon can throw them off, and either scare them, or bore them, because they won't understand what you're referring to.

- **Get them acquainted with the basic terms:** Meanwhile, hook them up with some very simple videos and easy-to-read books, on network marketing, so that they develop some understanding of their field. This will also help them perform better.
- **Simplify your ways of explanation:** Because there could be people from different walks of life, who may or may not have been trained to figure things out or problem-solve, you need to explain things simply. You should give them easy scenarios and examples to understand something easily. Take a basic and simple approach while explaining their tasks.
- **Be as defined and detailed as possible:** Your enrollees haven't done this before, so they don't know the nitty-gritty of network marketing. You need to be very detailed, in your explanations, don't skip things that may be trivial to you. The same things maybe very big obstacles to them. Your instructions should be well understood by anyone and everyone. For example, if you want them to put up a post on Facebook, make sure you tell them where to post. Explain the difference between group and personal posts and everything related to Facebook posts before you expect them to get this done.
- **Get them excited about not getting rejected:** It is important to remember, they fear rejection. They fear putting themselves out there. You need to develop a positive mindset,

letting them know it will go well. Get them excited to get on social media and attract viewers.

3. Harness the power of social media and get your enrollees started on their journey

As discussed in the previous chapters, social media is the most powerful tool at your disposal to make your business successful in every way! Your enrollees need to understand this, even those who have not used social media before or are not confident on social platforms. It may be very difficult for most, and they might fail more times than you can imagine. But you need to be with them every step, just like you were with yourself, when you kept on failing.

Also, you need to make this journey easy for them. They may not have the same level of understanding about posts, videos, or social media engagements. You need to break these down for them into easy to manage tasks each day, that they can do.

Ask them to find their niche: this is the next step that they can do once their story and goals are defined. There are several small steps, to get this done.

- **Note all the pain points:** For example, someone who figured that their story related to this product, was their weight loss journey, can just google the term "weight loss struggle" and find articles on this. They can now make a note of all the struggles that people who want to lose weight, go through. They can now use these "pain points" to interact with prospects.
- **Find relevant hashtags online:** Once the

information is gathered, they can search for relevant hashtags, on Instagram. In this case, "weight loss journey," "weight loss struggle," and so on.

- **Find their tribe:** They need to find a group of people who share the same situation, as they did, before using the product. This can be done by seeing who all on Instagram follows these relevant hashtags. This is their tribe, a.k.a, their target audience, for selling the product.
- **Note how this product can help these people:** before interacting with their tribe, your enrollees need to have a clear idea of how this product can be helpful to others. Your enrollees need to use this information and the pain points to make a convincing story.
- **Create content:** now, your enrollees are ready to create content. They can start by creating curiosity posts that will attract their audience to the content. They should surely use the relevant hashtags to ensure that their content reaches their target audience.

4. Offer them easy solutions to get their tasks done

Despite doing everything I have mentioned untill now, you may find many of your enrollees failing. As they fail, their motivation plummets, and they inch towards leaving, this. Remember, you are the captain of this boat. You need to help them make this work.

You need to provide them with easy-to-follow and effective strategies they can use as they start. Getting some positive results will help them retain their motivation levels and keep them from giving up.

If they tell you they spend long hours working on social media but are still not getting leads, they may be stuck in the "scroll hole." That is, they indeed open social media and are active for hours, but they keep scrolling and trying to find information, rather than taking action.

5. Help them find a balance

So, while your enrollee begins their social media marketing strategies, one thing that can ruin all their efforts, is their desperation. They must not seem desperate to sell the product when interacting with their prospects. They need to balance the tone of integration. It should be friendly and confident. Here are three strategies to close your prospect deals without seeming desperate:

- **Reach out effortlessly:** Start the conversations in a very natural way. Don't send direct messages that are more like advertisements, about the product.
- **Stop focusing on whether they are buying your product or not:** Stop focusing on the result, no matter how badly you need to close this prospect, it should not be evident, from your words. Make sure that they know you have their best interests at heart and that you are not doing this for your interest, alone.
- **Don't rush your customer:** Don't keep trying to sell the product. Don't push them to buy it, listen to them, listen to their problems,

and interact with them as naturally as possible.
This will increase their interest in the product.

As we all know, this can quickly become addictive even before you realize it. Maybe this is where they are stuck and need to start taking serious actions. Make sure not to overwhelm them with ten things to do to fix this, instead, you can suggest to them this simple but effective strategy below.

Daily Method of Operation

I like this method my team and I have implemented. To make your enrollees' active hours on social media productive, they need to have their 'Daily Method of Operation,' which is what they need to do, once they log in, to their social media accounts. These tasks need to be well-defined and executed within 36 hours to see results. They must finish these tasks every day for the people who comment, react, share, or follow them on their posts. These people are leads you attracted from your content.

Give Compliments: The ultimate truth is that people want appreciation. In our daily lives, each one of us feels at some point that we are underappreciated. Giving compliments can be a very positive note of starting an interaction with one of their followers. Your enrollees should aim to give three compliments in a day. This means they are at least positively engaging with leads through their platform. And because their social media handles have information about their business and products, these leads can very well get interested in it.

Send Out Private Messages: No, I don't mean that your enrollees should randomly start sending private messages on Instagram or Facebook. They should do it in steps. Stories are a great Instagram and Facebook feature to start interacting with those who follow your stories. Follow them back and send reactions or a short message (not related to the product or business) about this story. For example, if they are putting up a story about how difficult sticking to a diet is, your enrollee can share their experiences with it. This starts a conversation that builds the platform to sell your product in time

2-3 days: Your enrollees need to do this within 2-3 days only, with each person, and they will surely start seeing the results. Once they do, their experience and confidence in interacting with people and starting conversations will increase and help them move ahead.

If your enrollees are scared to begin this Daily Method of Operation, remind them that one doesn't need to have amazing skills, to grow their influence over social media. They just need to be sure of their story, goal, and trust in the product.

Finally, you need to make sure that your enrollees are in the correct mindset, that they are not expecting quick and easy money with this. You need to remind them, that there's no shortcut to becoming a successful network marketer, that it takes a lot of dedication, demanding work, and commitment.

What if your enrollees mess up the interaction with prospects? What if their approach is something that turns off the prospects, rather than getting them interested? How can you fix this? Can this be fixed? Don't worry, we will tackle all these questions and more in the next chapter.

4

Cultivating Great Relationships Virtually and Offline

The fact that you have decided to launch your network marketing business, is a great decision. This is because you now have the full power of social media that you can harness in separate ways to leverage your business. We have already covered some of these strategies in the last chapter, the real utility of social media is not using it to sell your product. It is to build relationships with your viewers, prospects, and clients.

Honing your people skills will allow you to develop and retain trustworthy relationships, with your clients. You need to understand the nature of this relationship before you even begin. You need to know what you should aim for and how you can achieve it in terms of customer relationships.

Let us say there's Anne, who owns a business of weight loss supplements, and your business is the same. Her profile on social media has the same number of followers as yours though the amount of engagement on her profile is higher! But her product is all the rage over social media, her sales are going up every day, and it's evident.

So, does that mean her product is better than yours? Who knows! That's for the customers to decide. But what is surely better in Anne's case is that she has a higher engagement. That does all the trick. Her followers relate to her posts. They engage in her posts, comment on them, and start conversations. Her followers then soon turn into prospects and then into clients.

So, with the same number of followers on social media, Anne can have 70% more customers than you. This is because Anne knows how to build customer relationships and how to make them last.

In network marketing, no matter how life-changing your product is, you can never close the prospect if they don't know you or trust you. Acing this part of the business will also allow you to train your enrollees in the right direction. You and your enrollees' efforts will then cumulatively grow your business.

The following five parts of the chapter will tell you all you should know and do to cultivate great relationships virtually and offline to make your business successful.

Part 1: How to Start a Conversation With a Prospect

You may be an introvert, extrovert, or ambivert. You may be fearful of under sharing or oversharing with your clients. You may have no idea how to start a conversation, over social media, with random strangers.

In any case, you or your new enrollees will face several challenges while starting a conversation with their prospects.

Starting a conversation sounds simple. It is an everyday task that everyone does. We begin many conversations daily with the supermarket cashier, the salon guy, your family, and your friends. But none of them feel daunting. This is because, in none of these conversations, there exists a pressure of making it work and closing a deal. In network marketing, every virtual conversation with your followers is a chance to make a sale, this is what makes these conversations so difficult.

But you remember that 'every human on this planet has at least one successful relationship.' Think of the one good relationship you have built in your life. If you have done that, you can do this too. (Metzger,2021)

Unlike real life, starting conversations over a virtual platform is comparatively easier. Imagine having to do this by walking up to someone in the middle of the street! Scary, right?

So, you already have technology backing you up. There's no need to ensure that you look clean and well dressed; there's no need to maintain good body language. You can talk with your client while you have pancakes in bed, which is fine. It's an easy deal; anyone can do it if they know how.

Remember, don't try to sell your product after two lines of text. That is a total turnoff, and this is something that Anne isn't doing for sure. You need to talk to your prospects and listen to them objectively. You must remember that even if you don't close this prospect today, you will learn. You will learn about them and their struggles, which will enrich your experience in network marketing. If you can't turn them into clients, it's okay because sometimes, they will lead you to someone else who may become a loyal customer. You never know.

A effective way to practice this, is to upgrade the Daily

Method of Operation from the last chapter. In addition to giving 3 compliments to, at least, 10 people for 3 days, try to learn 3 things about that individual through a conversation. You can decide what you learn about them. You can approach them with a simple compliment and get the conversation started. Following this, you can ask them 3 things, three questions you would like to know about them.

No, not questions like where they stay, what's their favorite band, or their favorite food. Ask them 3 open-ended questions. Show them that you're interested in getting to know their opinions on certain things, Don't even talk about your business. Just talk to them, get them interested, and let them ask you questions. Practice the power of 3 every day, and you will see things change.

No matter which stage you're stuck at right now, this will get you out of it.

Yes, I know it matters to close prospects, make the sale and earn your money. But the key to long-term success is holding back. Those who know this trick and apply it daily in their interactions are the ones who make progress. Slow and steady, but progress, nonetheless.

Part 2: Be Vulnerable

So you have put the daily method of operation into practice and reach out to ten or more people daily. You start conversations and talk for 5 minutes, but your messages go unread and unanswered. Or they asked you something in return, and you don't know whether you should answer, whether it's okay to take the conversation forward despite not being able to bring up your business. This makes you anxious.

You leave the conversation hanging and lose a prospective client.

This is a common situation that many of us face. Yet, no one tells you how to tackle this. No one tells you what's the right thing is, to do.

You may not like my advice here, but this advice comes from years of experience, trials, and errors. You need to open up to them, even if it means vulnerability. So when they ask you questions, you must answer them honestly, even if your answers reveal your weaknesses. Our weaknesses make us human.

While asking those 3 questions you had planned, you may think you are in control of the conversation. But you need to be ready for any questions that come your way. You must be honest, be vulnerable and raw in sharing your struggles. Most of us believe that people will trust us if we tell them how we have succeeded in the network marketing business. But it's just the opposite. People bond through sharing struggles and pain.

If you expect to talk to them about their pain points so that you can pitch your product, you will need to share them, too. Be open to sharing parts of your story, that you ideally wouldn't. People will continue the conversation or text you back the next day, when they find similarities with you and understand that you have been through some struggles as well. This is when, somewhere down the line in the conversation, you can talk about how the product has changed your life (your story about the product, remember?).

Well, practically speaking, the conversation with everyone may not be this straight forward all the time. You may need to talk about a ton of things before you reach the point where you make the pitch. But trust me, this is the only and most effective way of building client relationships. Building such relationships is important because your impression will last in their minds, even if they don't buy the product then and there. Later, when they struggle in life, they might contact you and show interest. This chance someday, sometime is equivalent to closing a prospect.

Allow yourself to make mistakes along the way, try different things, but keep going. Keep connecting to at least ten people every day in a natural way. Have heart-to-heart conversations and build a network. This network will be your strength in network marketing. You can tap into this network occasionally and see if they have developed an interest in making the purchase, or maybe they know someone who may need your product.

No matter what, build relationships with people, over social media, it's worth it. It will be your asset moving ahead, irrespective of whether they buy your product or not.

You need to remember that people are afraid to fail, but the only ones who fail are those who don't try.

Part 3: But How Vulnerable Should You Be?

The last two parts apply to both new enrollees and network marketers who aim to become leaders, in their field.

But this part is especially meant for network marketers who are leading a team and already have enrollees in their business.

We talked about vulnerability in the last section and how it is important to allow yourself to be vulnerable, if required, in front of your prospects.

You may think this is only applicable to your customer relationships, but it's not so. This is a universal approach for any business based on human networks, and it applies to every interpersonal relationship, in the network marketing business. You must have honesty and vulnerability while interacting with your team members, prospects or customers.

This is a blindspot, most leaders don't recognize it. Leaders, in general, don't want to be vulnerable. They believe that allowing themselves to be vulnerable reduces their authority as a leader, and their team members will stop respecting them.

Now, this mentality pulls one back from becoming a leader, more than you can realize. You might want to behave like you're unphased, you have everything under control, you don't want them to know that you struggle. No matter your internal state, you want to put on a mask of perfection and set an example for the rest of your team. You want them to become perfect, too. You know that there are a lot of struggles and shortcomings hidden behind this mask of perfection. Unbelievably, your team members will relate more to your shortcomings than your success. This is because they have shortcomings, too, and they are not as successful as you are. (Heilig, 2020)

"Credibility isn't perfection, it's the willingness to accept imperfection" ~ John Maxwell.

So the only relatable point between you and your team is the struggles you both have faced and are facing. Show them your flaws, scars, and problems. If you always talk about your success, they won't be interested. You want to live a scripted life on social media full of perfect moments that reflect a smooth upwards journey in your business, but they know it isn't real. This is because struggles exist, and they are facing them, now. They will not trust you if they believe you haven't had any failures in your journey. You can't be a leader if they don't trust you. Remember, when an enrollee signs up for your business, they join you and not your business.

They won't buy your success until they know about your failures. Without opening up, you will lose the connecting thread with your team. They will put you on a pedestal, sure, but they will also find you as someone unapproachable for their issues, which might seem trivial to them.

You cannot influence them in anyway until you share your struggles. Share the lessons you have learned on your journey and empower them to overcome their struggles. Just like you did. Set a realistic example of success, for them, a success that comes after multiple failures. With this, they will see themselves in you. This will make you a leader in the true sense, a leader who recognizes and knows their struggles. So remember to be vulnerable and open up about the failures and difficulties you have faced along the way.

Part 4: Don't Abandon Your Team

Again, this part is for those of you who want to become leaders, you need to take your team, along with you, on your journey. Ensure you are not abandoning them along the way.

On any given day, if you feel disappointed with something in the business and you express it negatively, your team will feel negative too. Remember, as a leader, you are in a position of authority, all of your actions and reactions transcend your team members. Your negativity will echo in their work and approach, that day. If someone in the team lets you down, you need to provide the solutions, so that they can rectify them. If you keep dismissing team members, when they make a mistake, you will have no one to progress this business with.

You will need to provide replicable solutions at every step of the way, no matter how many mistakes your enrollees make. Show them what you want from them, by setting an example. Show them, that these problems are solvable and how you would solve them.

The power of duplication will kick in, and they will start solving their problems, as opposed to losing motivation in their work, due to some negative remarks from you.

You need to show them how it's done, but you need to do this without putting any pressure on them. I know this sounds tricky, but you will find the balance with a few trials and errors. The most important thing is, to remember the strategy "don't abandon your team" and to have a positive approach toward problem-solving.

Part 5: How To Build A Personal Relationship And Why It Is Important

Many of you may feel this is too much abstract work to build a successful business. Why should you, an entrepreneur, spend time talking and sharing with people rather than making sales and earning money?

But in network marketing, human relationships, a.k.a, human networks are everything. That's why it's called "network" marketing. You need to focus on building the network first and marketing your product, second. Build a relationship before you jump to sell your product. The relationship is going to help you build everything, on top of it. It is the vehicle to carry all your assets, in this business.

Here is a guide to building successful interpersonal relationships, for network marketing:

- **Build a relationship of mutual trust and support:** It will start with giving compliments when you follow the Daily Method of Operation, of starting a conversation, for prospecting. Beyond the compliments, as you progress through the conversation, you need to develop mutual trust and support. Sharing your struggles and bonding over your pain points is a terrific way of achieving this.
- **Practice active listening with keenness:** Every one of us wants someone who listens with genuine interest. Don't give half hearted reactions or answers, while talking to your prospect. Even if you are talking with 2 or 3 prospects simultaneously, give them undivided attention. This strengthens their trust, in you, on a personal level. Overall, how will they trust your product if they don't trust you?
- **Show unadulterated interest in others:** You should continue on the conversation and show real interest in getting to know them. If only you do this, your prospects will also show interest in getting to know you. It is only then, you can pitch your product and talk about this business which is a major part of your life. Thus, showing unadulterated interest in others, can play out for your benefit.

- **Be a giver more than a receiver:** At times, when you don't find the space to pitch the product, wait patiently, continue your efforts, and give your prospect the time to talk to you. Listen to them and actively engage in the conversation. By doing this, you become distinguished from others because you listened patiently. This will strengthen your position in their lives, as a trusted friend.
- **Don't have unrealistic expectations:** Don't have expectations of things going smoothly and making high sales every day, even if it took less time with your last prospect. Don't base your expectations on previous activity. Every person is different and so are your chances of closing every prospect. Start with a clean slate, with every new prospect.
- **Be consistent in your efforts:** It may become tiring along the way. You may be desperate to make the sale and see results. Time may not be on your side. You need to wait it out while putting in consistent efforts. The difference between successful and unsuccessful leaders is consistency.

Your experience with each prospect will be different, and so will your success in turning them into clients. But if you take care of these actions, while interacting with your prospects, you will never have an unproductive day, in your network marketing journey.

If you're still unsure about how these relationships can have a direct impact on your business, here are a few of the benefits of having personal relationships with your prospects-

1. It will transform your leads into prospects and prospects into customers
2. Your prospects will trust you and spread the word on your behalf
3. These relationships will help you retain customers through your business
4. These relationships will give you friendships beyond business

Network marketing is a business that is mostly built upon interpersonal relationships. Now, interpersonal relationships in business need to be developed within your team and among your team and clients. Remember, you are the leader and hence you need to set the example of cultivating great relationships. If you're someone with social anxiety, yet strive to become a leader, don't let your social shyness get in the way. Be a keen listener and take an active interest in what your team members and your prospects have to say.

Bond with your teammates by being vulnerable, share your struggles, and showing them you are approachable and interested to guide them. However, through all these steps, remember to maintain the line of professionalism and don't overstep any boundaries. Don't feel overwhelmed as it's not as difficult as it sounds once you begin.

There are going to be so many different people on your team, with different aspirations and mindsets. Isn't it impossible to build healthy interpersonal relationships, with so many different team members? Well, not if you follow our team organization strategies coming up in the next chapter!

5

Building Team Culture

You may feel almost accomplished by the time you reach this chapter. Why? Because you already have enrollees in your business, using the strategies in the last chapter, and they have started to stick around! I mean, wasn't that the toughest part of becoming a leader?

Sorry to burst your bubble, but no!

So even if people are ready to be on your boat with you and follow you through a storm, it doesn't guarantee that you will get through the storm!

This is because it takes "teamwork" to successfully brave through testing times together as a team.

If there is no sense of "oneness" within your team, people will still leave and hop onto other boats when the ride gets tough.

There's a big chance of this happening even if you have successfully trained your enrollees in the correct direction. The reason is, every team member in your business (a.k.a enrollees turned team members) have their own struggles, on this journey. Without active interaction, with other team members, they may never feel a sense of belonging.

A sense of belonging, for us humans, is quite a primal feeling; whether it's our personal or professional lives, we all like to feel that we are at the right place, that the team is motivated, and is working for a cause. You're wrong if you think giving them matching t-shirts and company merchandise will cut it. Things in the real world run deeper than this, and we will explore the human psyche to real-life strategies, in this chapter, to make it work for you as a business leader.

Well, you may be clear about why you want to make your business work, you want to be a leader in this field, or maybe you want to change peoples' lives with your product!

But what about your team members? What is the one thing that binds them together and makes them work as one? What will make them look beyond their successes and work towards a successful business?

The answer is straight and simple: a positive and motivating team culture.

Now, this has a lot to do with your team members individually. But, as a leader, it is, ultimately your job to find prospective enrollees, get them trained, and bring all of them together, as a team.

To make your business flourish, you would need them to work as a team. There is no other way.

This is tough for two reasons- every enrollee is motivated to succeed on their own, and every enrollee will have their struggle. Most of all, there is a common problem- connecting through virtual meetings only. You may have team members based in distant locations, and it's only possible to interact via virtual meetings.

As if zoom calls weren't already confusing!

Not to get you anxious, but multiple things can go wrong and your enrollees can cancel out each other's progress, resulting in no business profits.

Realistically, you will have to tackle things better. As a leader, it's your job to knit your team together and combine their strengths, so they all work in the same direction, ensuring your business success.

In this chapter, this is what we will explore keeping those people on the boat from jumping off to another boat so that you can successfully brave the storm.

The Golden Rule of Deciphering Your Team

To build an effective team culture that works, you need to understand who all make up your team and their personality. Now, you may know them by their names or how they look in general, but that's not what I am talking about. You need to know their psyche and how motivated they are to work and take this business forward. Remember, at this point, we are not differentiating between personal aspirations or looking beyond working for the team.

At this point, we want to dive into their general aspirations and how much persistent efforts they put in to make their aspirations come true.

So, there exists a golden rule of 80/15/5 to decipher this. This is a golden rule because it never fails, no matter how new or old your business is, no matter the size of your team. This golden rule applies to any and every enterprise (Higdon, 2020).

Based on this rule, at any point in time, your entire

team can be categorized into three groups: 80%, 15%, and 5% people based on their level of aspiration. You may be guessing (and secretly hoping) to let the 80% be the high aspirants, the motivated and driven lot who will do everything to take your enterprise forward.

Alas, that's exactly what is not going to happen.

In reality, 80% of your team consists of people with low or no aspiration or motivation. Most of your company's volume, comes from those who aren't here for the money. They are just here to belong in a group and feel like a part of something. Money may be second or third on their list. The first is the sense of belonging.

Also, somewhere within this spectrum are people who are here to consume your product. That's because they like your product, they are interested in it and they want to have the benefits of free samples, once they become a part of your business. People such as them are scattered in varying proportions within your team, and for them the deal is simple— work, be a part of a team and also enjoy freebies!

Then, at the other end of the spectrum are the 5% of your team's members: this is the rare bunch. These are the ones who are motivated, put in lots of personal attempts, and go the extra mile to get things done. They are thirsty to earn the maximum amount of money possible, from this work. This level of desire, a.k.a aspiration, is great for them as well as you because these are the people who are driving your business forward. But, like it or not, there are only five people like this out of 100!

Finally, the remaining 15% of your team, these people are a buffer between the high aspirants and low (or no) aspirants. The people in this category have aspirants that are not sky-high but realistic, one can say. They are happy with taking $2,000-$3,000 home. Maybe because this is a side hustle, for them, or they don't want to put in too much effort. No matter the reason, this 15% of your team keeps the pace consistent for your business.

Thus, with this knowledge of the golden rule, you can now easily identify your team members. You can measure their level of aspiration in numbers, but you can take stock of their efforts. The level and intensity of their efforts should be a good identifier for their group type.

How to NOT build a Team Culture

So, at this stage, you have a good understanding of who all in your team make the 80%, and who makes the 15%. You have successfully identified high aspirants and low aspirants. But what to do with your new enrollees? Your new arrival team is going to be a mystery. To understand who among them belongs to which category, you would need to observe them for enough time to gauge their efforts. Do you have that time? If you keep observing every new arrival team just to make up your mind about their aspiration levels, if you wait that long to harness their skills for your business, how will your business ever move forward?

There must be a way to sort out the members of your new arrival team quickly and effectively and integrate them into the company. Yes, there indeed is, first, we will consider what you should avoid doing with your new arrival team.

As they say, prevention is better than cure.

If you think applying the golden rule to your new arrival team is the best way to get going. You are wrong.

Here are five scenarios that will tell you why. These scenarios are also what you want to avoid in your team. So get a notepad if you need one and read on—

Scenario 1: You're not sure about where your new team members stand in the level of aspiration, so you put all of them in the 80% category. You put them in the same room as the 80% of low (or no) productivity people.

Now, this is bound to fail.

Remember how excited your new enrollees tend to be? You've launched them to the moon, and they are ready to leap at you. Whereas the team members in the 80% are well integrated into the enterprise (they like their sense of belonging) but don't put in any effort to make things happen and don't care about the money. Well, once in a few months, they close on a prospect.

For the new team, 80% is a dangerous category to be around. As these people have no personal attempts at production, they become cynical, over time. This cynicism transfers to your new team members and even the most motivated, amongst them, become negative.

Well, to 80% of the team members: "If you're not working, we don't want your opinion." Thus, don't even put them in a position where they can pass on their opinions, blatantly. In short, keep the new arrival team away from the people in the 80% category.

Scenario 2: Now that you know of the hazards of placing your new team into the 80% category, you must do the opposite: you place your new team with the 5% of high aspirants. This, my friend, is bound to fail, as well. Here's why: your new enrollees are excited sure, they are motivated, of course, but are they ready to work 15 hours a day and put in 200% effort, like the members of the 5% category, to make it work? The answer is a big NO. They will either get intimidated or disappointed. It's common to be insecure when someone starts a new venture or job. Working with 5% of overachievers will surely overwhelm, your new team members. They may get disappointed for not being able to keep up with the 5% members. The result from this is also the same: your new members will become demotivated and negative. As opposed to what you want, they will feel out of place and doubt their abilities, to get things done.

Scenario 3: So, you decide it's unimportant, it's best to place your new team members with the middle 15%, who have an average level of aspiration. This should suit your new team members, right? Err, no! This is the worst category to be placed. This is because the members of this category are limited. They don't do much. They don't do less. They just do enough to make an average amount of money each month. This sets a disappointing example for your motivated new team members who have high aspirations (but aren't ready to put in the work yet). In this category, with the present 15% members, will crush their aspirations and make your business feel like any other side hustle or 9 to 5 job, to them. The result? Quite the same disappointment and negativity.

Scenario 4: This one is completely from our personal experience, there was a time in our business we felt we were doing everything, on behalf of our team, the result? We were drained. Moreover, people would reach out to us to help them do a business presentation or talk about a product. These were people that would have been in the business for a long time. We wondered why they still had to call us when they knew how to do it. We couldn't take on these requests, because we were swamped with work already. Then, it occurred to us that we never showed our team or business partners, how to use the free virtual tools given by our company. They thought that people needed to hear it from us, so they could get convinced. Little did we know that our personalities don't duplicate, but the tools do. So when we realized that was the problem we showed our people how to use the tools (presentations, presentations videos, video testimonials, and our company's app) to make it duplicatable and have them do it, on their own.

Scenario 5: Another one from a load of our past experiences; a common mistake we made as beginners, was getting stuck with the same sales volume. When this happened, we immediately switched to management mode. We started calling our leaders and telling them what to do so they start being productive. This was wrong, because we as a leaders, weren't being productive either. We realized that we can not control what others do, but we can control what we can do, to grow our business. We learned that the pace of the leader is the pace of the team. So, when we became leaders, we made it a point to set an example, for our team. If people see us doing what we want them to do, they will get inspired. So we care about our leaders and love them very much, but we learned not to push them (remember the level of desire?). If they didn't want to work it was ok, we started building new teams. When they saw us recognize the members of the new team, some were jealous and wanted our time, again. They did what was required to get it an that is take action. After we did this our team grew and our sales volume grew even more.

These are all the scenarios that you need to prevent

from taking place with your new team members. Read on to learn about strategies that you can apply instead.

Delivering the Sermon

Well, keeping the motivation up in your entire team and boosting their working impulse, is much like delivering a sermon at church. Remember, church days from childhood when you would have to sit and listen to Sunday sermons? Depending on how much money you seeded, were you treated differently? Did you receive a different sermon? No. The message was the same, assuming that there are different people to whom the sermon appeals, differently. These sermons may have been the guiding light for another child and you, maybe not so much.

Similarly, you deliver motivating speeches and hold team meetings: for some, it may boost their productivity, for others, it may not. You need to face this reality and accept it.

This applies to your new team members as well as the past team members. The sermon for all is the same, who is inspired by it and who doesn't is something you can't control. Now desires change through time, of course, there will be more for those who are curious, those who raise their hands and ask questions, in the meetings, and those who seek more guidance. You will guide them more thoroughly when they ask for it. But, until someone raises their hand, you need to treat your entire team at the same level.

Well, you may think that the golden rule of 80/15/5 is the basis of building a team culture within your enterprise. It's rather ,the opposite. The 80/15/5 rule is to understand your team's composition. You, as a leader, need to be aware of your team's psyche and keep the 80/15/5 compartmentalization, to yourself. It's for your reference to understand and find ways to make your business successful with this composition.

Tips For Effectively Building a Team Culture

The last two sections tell us that you shouldn't differentiate your new team members into any 80/15/5 groups. Don't use any segmentation ('cause it will make them negative), rather, give them a challenge. Give them a chance to prove their capabilities and find their position in the company. Here' is how you can do it.

Put all your new team members in a temporary group. Give them a challenge, within 10 days, get 1 new customer, if they complete the challenge successfully, they get into the Qualifier Group.

Now, this challenge should be open to your current team members, as well. This will give the 80% members to put in some effort for, maybe, the first time that year, the 15% will fit this in for their monthly target of $2000-$3000, the 5% will do this because they do everything.

The chances are most of your team members, will be able to meet this challenge because most of them have the experience.

For your new team members, it will be a chance to prove themselves, irrespective of their level of desire.

Overall, this is, a solution where everyone benefits, because you will gain new customers as well as have all your team members, new or old, working in the same direction.

This is one of the ways to build a team culture with members with different aspiration levels and keep the culture alive, when new members join in. With experience, you will find more ways to make this happen.

How to Lead A Volunteer Army

Giving your team members a challenge and then forgetting about the rest of it, is not the way to go. You become a leader with consistent efforts and by practicing leadership skills. You need to know effective ways of leading an army of volunteers, new team members, or your enterprise. Use the following methods to sharpen your skills and flourish as a leader. Here, are 5 things that you should practice deliberately and consistently to build a team culture, and to lead your team members towards success, no matter how well, or worse, your business may be doing (Premier on Demand, 2019).

- Give direction:

Ask your team members, what's their purpose, and why have they joined your business. What do they hope to get out of it? Your purpose may be clear as a leader, but are all your team members clear on it? Without a sense of purpose, they wouldn't know which direction they should be moving towards. If they want to make more money, they should focus on closing more prospects, if they want to overcome their social anxiety, they should be working on social media marketing. Without direction, your team can not be successful in any way.

- Give clarity:

Make sure that all your team members are clear about what is expected of them. Don't make your team members wait for a task and wait for their turn to prove themselves. In a team, if there's a lack of clarity, team members quickly lose interest, and become demotivated. As a leader, it's your task to define their roles in the business and give them clear targets to meet. This allows everyone to make progress without getting in each other's way. A clear outline of expectations.

- Give responsibility:

Many leaders make this mistake. As leaders, seldom do we want to share our responsibilities, we take the burden of the world, on our shoulders, and try to fix everything, ourselves. As discussed, in the last chapter, this has a lot to do with being vulnerable as a leader. It is important to be vulnerable and hand the microphone to your team members sometimes. This will help in releasing others, into their potential, and making the best of their potential.

- Give encouragement:

Don't underestimate the power of encouragement. Notice when others do good and call them out on it, appreciate them, for their efforts. Remember, "what's rewarded is repeated." Shout-outs are an amazing way to get this done. In team meetings, appreciate and encourage people in front, of the entire team. This simultaneously encourages the achievers and inspires those who are still trying.

- Give feedback

No, your task as a leader, doesn't end with encouraging, even more important is to provide constructive feedback, to your team members whenever and wherever necessary. Address any issues, quickly, before things get out of hand and show them how they can overcome these issues.

As a leader, your job doesn't begin or end, anywhere. It's a 24/7 job that you must keep, as long as, you want to be considered a leader.

To be honest, much of your inherent skills, as a leader don't come from running a business, they arise from other situations. For example, if you have ever led a team, let us say in your church, managing the choir or the Board of Trustees. Otherwise, if you have ever led a team for volunteer activities, you may already know what you need to keep your team motivated and united. This is because, when you're working towards a common goal with a team, you can't fire or hire new people, you must learn to work with everyone.

You will naturally be forced to learn how to lead and inspire and partner for a common goal. There is an entire book dedicated to this- 'Making the First Circle Work: the foundation for duplication in Network Marketing by Randy Gage and this talks in depth about the growth of a leader from their daily experiences.

Benefits of Being Involved in Network Marketing

Well, it sure does seem like a lot of work, but network marketing has several benefits. Your team needs to understand these benefits clearly. Incentives and benefits are a terrific way of keeping up the team's motivation. You need to help them realize that network marketing is not only about a product, service, or compensation plan, but it's also all about relationships, friendships, community, and culture; it's about awesome events, feeling good, recognition, and acknowledgment (Pousson, 2019).

As a leader, if you want to make it big, you need to think about a mission that's bigger than the money. You need to think about how you can influence people and knit different people's skills together, to make one amazing team. You need to think about the community you want to build, the training you want to give to those who need it, the kind of work culture you want to build in your business, and the core values of your business, that you want to develop.

Takeaway:

To keep your business running efficiently, your teams need to be well functioning. When the new arrivals start to pour in, you would need a quick strategy to organize them into teams that would suit them the best. As a leader, you need to use the 80/15/5 rule for the dividing of your new and existing team members. You would also need to thoroughly follow the 5 steps given in the "how to build a volunteer army" section of this chapter to ensure that all your enrollees are well trained and most of all, motivated. Remember, that sometimes, leading a network marketing business is less about the business and more about building a cohesive community that gives you a sense of achievement.

Now, you are well equipped, with the "logic" of organizing your team members. You know all that you must do, and all that you must avoid. How do you exactly follow these "logics"? You need tools at your disposal to help implement these strategies. In next chapter, is our comprehensive take on how you can use a simple social media platform, to do most of the organizing and leading, virtually.

6

How to Use Facebook Group to Manage Your Team

Now that you're all set with your new enrollees and have started to find your footing, it's time to upgrade, to the next level! This level is all about growing your team, as well as, your business.

But first, it's always best to make your internal structure robust, before you move on to expand. With what is given in the last two chapters, you should be able to train your new enrollees, in the right direction and keep them from jumping off the boat.

The good news, you're almost through the storm, and it's getting calmer, the chaos has started to die, and there are no more immediate challenges to deal with.

The bad news, you don't know what to do now. If there was a storm to deal with, you had a clear goal– to get past the storm with your boat of people intact. Now that you're almost on the other side, with all the people you started with, now what?

Well, grow your business, silly! Make the most of your

business and aim for more clients, who are the source of your profit! The question remains, how exactly?

If you're still relying on your enrollees to follow the Daily Method of Operation to help you boom your profits....you're making a mistake!

Every level has its strategies. The daily method of operation works like a miracle when you're just starting, but once you've reached a steady level and your business starts to take off, you need to apply new strategies. This is when you must use the power of social media to the maximum!

Yes, social media is still your best friend for network marketing, but this time you need to harness the power of a specific social media platform, Facebook Groups!

Okay, I am not going to assume that all of us know what Facebook Group is, and you shouldn't as well. For those of you not aware of Facebook Groups, it's an extremely useful platform for network marketers, where you can build a community with people who are interested in your business.

How do you spot people who are genuinely interested in your business? How do you make them a part of your group? How do you even start a group?

Questions like these may be swarming in your head, but don't worry, this chapter is designed to help you make the most of Facebook Groups, for your business, and we will start right from the basics.

You may have already set up a Facebook Page, for your business, and you're happy with it, you post about your business, from time to time, and get average engagement. Where does this lead your business? How does this contribute to your outreach and your profits? A simple

Facebook page doesn't provide the space for active engagement, discussions, community building, or closing prospects. That's why Facebook Groups exist. A Facebook group can be public or private, hidden or visible, based on your choice. People who genuinely want to be a part of your community can join and integrate themselves, easily. A Facebook Group increases your outreach and improves your business statistics steadily, if you know how to use it.

The best way to know more about it? Of course, reading up on it (a leader needs the knowledge to lead)! Refer to the book "Social Media for Network Marketing Professionals" for the easiest guide to opening Facebook groups using an ATM system for effective team building.

How To Make Your Team Game Strong With Facebook Groups?

Before you think of using Facebook Groups to find more prospects and build a customer base, think of what you can do for your team through this platform. Growing your team through remote connections is one of the greatest challenges in network marketing, and Facebook Groups, can be a terrific way of overcoming that challenge.

Let's consider a person who doesn't have any know-how, about your business, and has just stumbled upon your Facebook Group. How do you draw that person in? As hypothetical as this scenario may be, it's important to understand that not everyone clicking on your Facebook Group, is a fan of your business. 80% of your engagement will come from people who don't know about it but think it's interesting. Your Facebook Group's job is to hook their interest and turn it into a genuine desire to join your business. Sounds tricky? Here are a few tips for you to interest any other person on Facebook about your business through Facebook Groups (Higdon, 2021).

- Help new visitors navigate through your page easily

First, if you want to grow your team members and want more enrollees to sign up, you need to think from their perspective. You need to make your Facebook group "new-user" friendly. Most groups, are filled with content and discussions that seem alien to a new person navigating your site. This makes them feel overwhelmed/underwhelmed/out of place, and they move on with their scrolling. Therefore, you need a dedicated section or page for new visitors or prospective enrollees.

Your banner should have a navigation button for new visitors only. Consider a button that says, "new to the page?" which will tempt them to click on it. This linked page, for new visitors, should be carefully tailored to help them understand your business and how they may fit in it. The overall vibe of the page should be very welcoming and easy to understand (and not overpacked with technical details), giving them a simple and interesting overview of what this group is all about.

- All Business and No Play lowers your chances of expanding

As a network marketing leader, it's natural to be focused

on your business and strategies. But, to someone who has just joined your Facebook Group, the dedicated page should reflect a fine balance between work and enjoyment. There are two reasons for this: first, not everyone is looking for money, not everyone wants to hustle their heart out and make a ton of money as soon as they begin; two: even those who are looking for money need to know that your team is a fun place to be, that they would get breathing space and would be enjoying their work. So, while you design a page for the newcomers, keep the fun content along with your serious business content.

- The law of relatability

In a day, hundreds of random people may visit your Facebook Group. Now, the best way to make them move ahead to the next step (enrolling in your business) is to hit them with "relatability" (not literally). This just means that your Facebook Group should make them feel like they belong there and would fit right in effortlessly. This would make them engage with you and not make your Facebook Group, just another page in their feed. In summary, don't think from a leader's perspective, but from a people's perspective.

- Find your team cheerleader

All the things I have listed might not be your strongest suit. Maybe you're an amazing leader but not much of an interactive person, don't do it yourself. Find someone in your existing team members and hand over the responsibility to them. There are a few pros to this decision, your chosen team member (or maybe they volunteered) knows exactly how to make your group Facebook Group interactive and fun (because it comes naturally to them); it will surely work out; you don't have to make an effort, and your existing team members can represent your business well.

Get Prospects With Facebook Groups: 10 Ways To Grow Facebook Groups Fast

From my personal experience, I have seen multiple Facebook Groups. They exist, but don't grow. These groups are like a dead log. They have the same number of members. More tend to leave than join, every day. Overall, the group is evident that things are going downhill. Now, who would like to engage with an already sinking boat? So, to prevent this negative cycle of people leaving and pulling down the overall reputation of your business, you need to keep some things in mind while using Facebook Groups (Simone, 2021).

Here are ten strategies for how you can tailor your Facebook Group to grow your business effectively.

Focus on building a community

Often, with all the targets and pending sales on our minds, we forget the pillar on which any network marketing business stands, the community. Of course, you will be doing your business through your Facebook Group. It is ultimately meant for that, but, first, you must focus on building a strong community of people who believe in your business and support it. People who cheer you on frequently, engage in your posts and are essentially "loyal" to the group. A community will make your Facebook group an exclusive entity and more people would want to belong to this "exclusive group" with a keen sense of community. Nothing binds people and keeps them together, than a sense of belonging. So, before you pitch your product or market it, focus on building a community of people, with common interests or common problems.

Build interpersonal relationships with people

Interact with your group members, be active, and remind them why they are a part of the group. It can be anything; make a good morning post, ask the members how they are getting through their Monday's, engage with the comments, and respond to them. Be chatty and listen to what the members have to say. Don't only make posts about your product, business, or profits; people don't care about that because it's not affecting them directly. Talk about daily and even mundane things from time to time. It will give people a reason to stay, in the group. The main takeaway, is if you listen to the people and engage with them, they will also listen to you when you talk, about your product, one day. It's a two-way street.

Be the expert in the group

This is a reminder from chapter 1. To be a leader, you need to be an expert, in your field. Your Facebook Group is a good platform to express your expertise and people will listen to and stick with you, when they believe you know your stuff. So, posting small tips and tricks from your knowledge trunk, is always ideal. Keep it short, to the point, and interesting. Don't make it like a lecture. Talk as if you would advise a friend. It's best to have a schedule for such content. For example, create a new tips and tricks video every Friday. This makes people tune into your group on regularly and helps them remember, about your business (in case they forget). This works well for both active members in the group and not-so-active ones.

Have dedicated welcome posts for new members on your group weekly

This is essentially important to increase the number of new enrollees and gradually expand, your team. So, any new person, in the group, might not be able to catch up on the ongoing topics or discussions, which may turn them off. An effective way to keep this from happening is "welcome posts," this is a post, video, or a Facebook live, every week for new people. This makes them feel integrated, recognized, and welcomed. Make sure to have an interactive post and engage with the newcomers.

Share testimonials and ask others to share

Now, it's time to start incorporating your product and business into the posts. A simple way of doing this (without losing their attention) is, by sharing testimonials. This positively impacts the members' thinking about the product. Of course, any individual new to the product or the business would have doubts, but listening to testimonials from existing team members or clients can help them feel more connected to the product. This also impacts the prospects in a dilemma about the product. A testimonial will provide them with a realistic view of the product and its efficacy. Remember to ask others to share their experiences in such posts, this will keep the ball rolling, and your post will always have engagement.

Interview experts on your product's review

One of the most common issues that keep people from finalizing their purchase is doubting authenticity. When a product is being marketed vigorously, it can lead to skepticism, among viewers. Some prospects may have more doubts than others. To overcome this, try to approach experts and ask them to share their reviews, about the product. Share this review in the form of an interview, article, or live video. Taking this step can improve your chances of closing, on most prospects.

Have a live every week with a tutorial or presentation or even launching a new product

Referring to point number 3, sharing your expert view, every week, may become a little repetitive for your members. If you spot this tendency (example: decreasing engagement on weekly lives) mix it up. Release videos every week but keep rotating your content. It can be a product launch, a tutorial, or a testimonial. Keep it real and interesting. Always ask your viewers to leave their thoughts, about the video, in the comments section and be engaged in the comments. This increases the traffic, to your content, steadily.

Promote your group on Facebook Live

Coming back to the members, of your Facebook Group and the sense of community (this is how you balance it out); to make your videos and live sessions, on Facebook, more than just promotional videos, for your business, promote your community, as well. Talk about your Facebook Group, in the videos and urge people to check it. Advise them about the benefits of being a member, (such as free tips and tricks, can be one). This makes people curious and sets a positive cycle in motion.

Link your group to your social media profile

This is how people know the importance of the community you have built in your life. Be sure to link your Facebook group to your social media handles. This gives people easy access to your group's page, ensuring people can follow you and become aware of your group and business. Bringing attention to your business, beyond your immediate social media family. The more the merrier.

What to avoid while using Facebook Groups

Since there was a strategy section, I will enlighten you all about the things you shouldn't do. Sometimes, even if you only know which direction to avoid, you can land on the correct path. So, here are 12 things that you should avoid while using Facebook Groups for your business (Sirona, 2018).

Do not over-schedule your posts on Facebook Groups

Like most things, there are two faces of the scheduled post feature on Facebook Groups. It's good to have scheduled posts for any latest content you may be posting after a while, to catch your members' attention, or to just let them know that you will be away, for a while. But scheduling your posts will separate the traffic on your group's page. With all posts scheduled at definite times, people will only tune in at those times, and you may see a decrease in the regular engagement. So never overuse the Schedule Post feature.

Don't urge your members to private message you

I'm sure all of us have had this frustrating experience of people asking us to "PM" them, for information. Never be that person if you want your business to succeed. Having a Facebook Group in place for your business gives the idea that you're here to share everything, including handling queries. If you publicly ask someone to "PM" you, for more details, two negative things happen in tandem, first, the person with the query feels frustrated about not getting a direct reply and second, it comes out as a lack of transparency, to your larger audience. Always respond to queries directly and openly, rather than asking them to message you privately.

Don't just share links without a little explanation and personalization

If you're posting and reposting content, to keep your group engaged, make sure you do so thoroughly. In other words, as you share the content add your thoughts about it, explain how it links to your business and share your expertise on it. Essentially, customize the posts and links before you share anything, on your Facebook Group. This will add credibility, to your business, and prevent people from getting confused about why this particular content is being shared in the group.

Don't cross-post directly

This is a little analytics secret that I am sharing with you. Facebook doesn't like redirecting its crowd to another link, so when you cross-post links from other platforms, Facebook won't show the entire content, only the link. This makes the content less accessible for your members. They can't see what the content, all they can see is a huge link you're asking them to click on!

To get through this Facebook caveat, you need to upload the video, of interest, separately and then post it to your group. You can use a screen recorder, on your mobile or laptop, to record the video and then upload it on Facebook. This will allow your members to see the content, easily, and restore trust in you and your post.

Do not constantly promote yourself and your company

As mentioned before, you need to keep the content diverse but relatable. Don't talk (or brag) constantly about your company, people will find it repetitive and or even irritating. Be community-oriented, take time to talk and discuss common pain points for members , and share solutions to overcome them. This is one example, you can just ask them to post their Christmas tree photos below yours, which may work perfectly.

You don't help and communicate with your members

This is a big no-no! Opening a Facebook Group only to make profits (which is the aim) and you want to achieve this by talking about your product continuously, without paying any heed to what people have to say or ask, it's never going to work! Growing your business is a winding road, you need to help people at every bend and corner to strengthen your chances of making any profit at all. Make sure to be there for your members, every way. This increases the bonding, creates a stronger community, helping people trust you and your product.

Your Facebook Group doesn't have any rules

Now that would be silly! Every group should have rules, otherwise, hell will break loose! Facebook is an open platform for all sorts of people. If you want your Facebook Group to function properly, you should have simple rules, for your group, posted clearly on the homepage. Make sure to implement the rules as well, otherwise, no one will take you or your group seriously.

You expect people to have common sense

This is a mistake that all of us keep on making and this can happen during your Facebook group journey as well. There will be people who try to steal your content, make money from it, or pester you for free stuff, for no reason. It's best to shake off these things as soon as possible and move on with your journey.

You're always serious and you don't have fun

This can be a serious letdown, for your audience. You may be a serious person, or you may be talking about a serious topic, no matter what, keep it interesting and engaging. Have fun, ask fun questions, or share fun things from your experiences. If you keep your content serious and dry, people will stop watching, as soon as they tune in. You don't want that, do you?

Stop adding people to your group without their consent

This can be irritating and give a negative impression about your company. No matter how desperate you want new members, never add people without their consent. This way, they would surely be suspicious and leave the group and in the worst case may report your group. This can result in severe damage to your group's reputation.

You don't preselect your members

For any Facebook group to be legit, it must have criteria and a pre-selection method. For example, have a simple survey with three basic questions about why they want to join the group and, based on the answers, allow them (or not) to become a member. This, again, screams exclusivity and makes your group appealing to people.

Your Facebook Group isn't private

You may think having a public Facebook group will attract more crowds. Well, there are numerous hackers and spammers in that crowd, as well. Do you want them to mess up your group's content and leak the data? Not ideal, right?

Make sure your Facebook group is private to keep the security of your content in place.

Adapt and evolve using Facebook groups for your business

Finally, once you have done all that is to do and avoided all that you should while making your Facebook Group, you might want things to grow naturally and keep pace. But unfortunately, that's not possible! To keep your Group alive in the test of time, you need to modify it, elevate it, and keep it relatable. When you stop learning or evolving, you will lose your business and your brand will fizzle out. You can lose money, if you don't know what you're doing or are not flexible. Keep up with your Facebook group. This is a long journey to keep your business booming and can get tiring. Keep in mind simple hacks, like teaching your new enrollee how to invite people to your group. You can invite every new follower you get to your Facebook group to ensure your group is growing and not dying a slow death.

Conclusion

To sum it all up, Facebook Groups are a powerful tool to expand your business. Make sure you focus on building a community first, and don't start selling your product immediately to every new group member. Make everyone feel welcome and have dedicated posts for newcomers. Keep it balanced with the fun stuff and the business stuff. Finally, don't take the security of your group lightly, keep your group private and preselect each member. There, you're all set to go!

Now you know how to build an online community, maintain and grow your team with it. But, what about those team meetings that are unavoidable? How do you make sure that everyone is on the same page and working efficiently and not just chilling in their pajamas at home. This is a virtual business! More on how to solve these common yet tricky situations in the next chapter!

7

Organizing And Managing Remote Interactions

Well, we have talked so much about strategies, in the last few chapters, what to do and what to avoid doing, but, in practice, all strategies fail if one thing isn't in place. That thing is team cohesion. If your team is not united as one, if they are all doing their own thing, you cannot expect your business to progress, let alone be profitable.

Everyone who gets into network marketing has their objectives and reasons for doing so. While it's particularly important to appreciate the personal journeys of your team members, it's equally important to bring them together and find common objectives (which can be idealistic as well) to work towards. Team cohesion is one of the greatest tasks of a leader. No one can substitute you for this role. You are solely responsible for knitting everyone together and keeping everyone together throughout the distinct phases of your business journey.

You might think that you have already done so, while recruiting new enrollees and giving them the necessary training, but alas! The job of a leader is incessant. After the recruitment, training, and integration into your business, your trainees need to know what they are working towards and with whom they are working.

Now, this wouldn't need an entire chapter if your business involved checking into an office- a common space, every day. In that case, they would naturally interact daily, and you wouldn't need to do anything about their coordination. However, in the world of network marketing, where communication through virtual platforms is key, the job of a leader is multifold.

You need to ensure that your team is on the same page, with the same frequency and same level of passion, for progressing this business. This can be a very tricky job to gauge each of your team member's levels of commitment, interest, and skills for the job. Keeping elevated levels of motivation consistently, will be a challenge.

All of this must sound very intimidating, but by the end of this chapter, you will gain lots of insight and constructive tips about managing your team's interactions through virtual platforms. In this is a chapter, you will want to take notes as well as start implementing into practice.

But first, how do remote meetings work?

For those who are not big on meeting people in person and putting in all the effort to dress up, show up on time, and have the perfect calm face while talking, remote meetings seem a blessing, at first. We stay in our home clothes, log in to the meeting, keep the camera off, put ourselves on mute, and let it run in the background while scrolling through social media. I am sure, some of us are guilty of doing at least one of these things and not dealing with remote meetings, seriously. But, when you're the one, who oversees of scheduling and managing these meetings, there is no shortcut to managing it remotely.

Before you panic, let me say that it's quite easy to navigate through remote meetings (for your nerves), and this chapter is your all-in-one guide to acing remote meetings for your team's cohesion. For now, if you know how to turn on a webcam, your mic and schedule a meeting on any app, you are ready to begin.

As a virtual network marketing leader, you need to use the potential of remote meetings to the maximum to help your business stay profitable and soar high. This means, you need to take remote meetings seriously and prepare for them. No more wearing pajamas to meetings or Scrolling on social media, while the meeting is on mute. If this list of doable has started to turn you off, let us replenish all the advantages of remote meetings for your business!

Top 10 advantages of remote meetings for virtual marketing

Reduced costs

This has to be the biggest payoff of remote meetings, reduced costs. In one shot, remote meetings take the costs of commuting, conference hall rents, and costs of maintaining an office off your list. Besides by a reduction in the personal effort of traveling (long or short distances), translating (most remote meeting platforms have translations), and manual scheduling (you can schedule meetings using one click on online platforms).

Moreover, it also saves time for everyone involved. No matter where your team members are located, they can just join in with a link. Remote meetings are super convenient and efficient way of conducting meetings.

Improved communication

When chartered well, remote meetings can become a platform for strengthening communication, within and across teams. Of course, it will be your job to encourage people talking and then redirect the conversations whenever required, but if it's done well, remote meetings can enrich all your team members. Your team members can share a common space (even though it's virtual) and communicate directly. This increases your teams' familiarity, solidarity, and comfort level with each other. The more they are acquainted, the easier your job gets to manage.

Saves time

Needless to say, the biggest perk of conducting meetings remotely, is saving time. The ease of scheduling, rescheduling, and keeping track of these meetings, saves everyone, especially the team leader, a lot of time. On average, scheduling a remote meeting, inviting everyone, takes less than 5 minutes. This scheduling time can be further reduced if you have your team lists with all email ids sorted beforehand. No matter how close your office could have been, nothing beats just 5 minutes of scheduling and 10 seconds of logging in to a meeting.

Boosts productivity

Remote meetings are much more efficient than in-person meetings, and here's why— during every in-person meeting there is a lag time, the time during which all the attendees arrive at the venue one by one, taking time to settle down and get up to speed. This lag time can slow down the start of the meeting and hinder the real effective time of the meeting, the time during which the important discussions happen. During a remote meeting, as soon as everyone joins in, with a click, you are ready to begin. No need to find your chair while the team waits to start.

Enhances cross-team collaboration

Have you ever tried to have cross-team meetings in a conference room? If you have, then you certainly know how messy it can get. If you haven't, you have saved yourself a lot of hassle. Despite the hassle, cross-team meetings are necessary, from time to time. Remote meetings can make your cross-team meetings more organized and efficient.

All online meeting platforms have their own chat box through which members can immediately address any queries, share information, and solve problems simultaneously, as the discussion continues. So, even when two members are talking, another member can post their comments, questions, or advice in the chat box (visibility of the chat box can be customized), without disrupting the meeting flow. Trust me. It doesn't get better than this.

Global talent pool

This is another obvious and very big advantage of remote meetings: the nullified distance. It doesn't matter if your team member is from another part of the world, on a continent with a 12-hour time difference, or living in the same city as you, if they are talented and interested in your business, nothing stops them from becoming team members.

Just imagine if you had to hire team members for an in-person office; based in Ohio. For example, you would never be able to sign up someone from South Korea, no matter how talented they are (maybe they don't want to relocate). With completely remote operations and meetings, distance is not a factor. Thus, you can easily have clients and team members from all over the globe. This is extremely beneficial for your business and helps your business to diversify.

Focused communication

No matter how fixed the agenda is for in-person meetings, there's always some deviation in the end. However, in remote meetings, you have more control. While a focused discussion is on, you can just mute comments for the time being. You can also request the attendees to put their queries in the chat box, which will be addressed at the end of the meeting. These options don't exist during face-to-face discussions in a room full of people. Remote meetings help you conduct focused communication while keeping distractions at bay.

Well-structured

Comparatively, remote meetings are way more structured than in-person meetings. During in-person meetings, digressions, people's comments, and reactions get in the way of the smooth progression of the meeting. In remote meetings, you can just go ahead with the plan and follow the structure of the meeting, even if people have comments or are distracted, it won't directly affect the meeting's progression. With remote meetings, it is possible to plan and maintain the structure of the meeting.

Success-oriented

This is what meetings are meant for, right? To solve problems in the way or to find new ways of moving towards success. Remote meetings are the best way to bring all your team members together and discuss strategies to help your business move ahead. This not only contributes to the individual success of your enrollees, but it also means the collective success of your business. It is a solution where everyone benefits.

However, if you try to keep the same mindset while conducting in-person meetings, it won't be this effective: for example, if someone is absent from the meeting, it affects everyone's morale, and they start thinking they could have bunked it too. But the effect of someone not showing up is not as pronounced during remote meetings. Thus, keeping up the motivation and inculcating a positive mindset during remote meetings is much easier.

Now that you're up to speed with all the benefits of conducting remote meetings for your team, you need to train yourself to manage these meetings. You may want to enjoy the benefits of online meetings by staying in your pajamas, attending meetings sitting on your couch while sipping on a pina colada, but when you're a leader, you just don't have the choice of doing these things. Because it's you who has to arrange the meeting, speak up first, set the agenda, and break the ice with every attendee. You are the make-or-break factor of these remote meetings. No attendee will take the meeting seriously if you're uncharged for the meeting and your body language is casual. To keep this from happening, you need to know certain "virtual meeting etiquettes" that will help you to conduct successful meetings without much hassle.

Virtual meeting etiquettes for effective communication (Miro, 2020)

Define the need

Before you even go ahead with setting up a meeting, ask yourself if a meeting is necessary. This is something many leaders forget to do. Remember, if the meeting is unnecessary in reality, your team members will find it a waste of time and be cynical every time you call a meeting. You want to avoid this, so before setting up any meeting, ask yourself the following questions-

- Can I solve this issue myself?
- Can I solve this issue without a meeting?
- Can this issue be solved, completely through a meeting?
- Can a process be created to solve this issue, without a meeting?

I am sure you have never thought this much before calling a meeting. These questions are extremely necessary as they define the need to have a meeting when you're sure there's no other way to solve it.

Limit the number of attendees

This is something no one does. Leaders feel that limiting the number of attendees for the meeting is counterproductive. However, inviting many people with little to do with the issue increases the deadweight of your meeting. To have a successful meeting, you need to invite only those who can contribute to resolving the issue and benefit from the discussion. You can use the responsibility assignment matrix to determine your team members' responsibilities and find the most suitable members for the meeting.

Pick the best timing for all the attendees

Often leaders are caught up in their schedules and forget to consider the convenience of their team members before scheduling a meeting. In a network marketing business, you will be working with people all across the globe in, different time zones. It may be difficult to figure out a time that works for everyone, but it's crucial. I suggest using a basic time zone to denote the time, such as GMT, and a form within which everyone can mention their preferred time.

Set a clear agenda

Step one of this process should have taken care of this for you, mentally. You should know why, this meeting is being held and why the selected attendees are invited, to the meeting. You also need to mention this clearly, in the meeting agenda. This transfers your motivation, for the meeting to your team members. Once they know why this meeting is taking place and how they can contribute to it (what would be their role), they will understand its importance.

Have all your tools prepared

As a leader conducting the meeting, you must check the online platform you plan to use beforehand. Whether it's Skype or Zoom, ensure you know all the features and their utility. You can also arrange for additional tools necessary for the meeting, such as poll taking, feedback forms, etc. It's always best to also have a plan B, for each tool in case any problem arises. This is how you can ensure the smooth functioning of the meeting.

Provide a virtual space to collaborate

While the meeting is on, make sure you have some shareable documents prepared where people can brainstorm and collaborate. Google sheets or google docs are efficient virtual spaces where people can write, edit, post comments, and resolve issues together. This enhances the outcomes of your meetings, multifold.

Introduce everyone and present your agenda

A remote meeting will never work if people are unaware of who is in the room (aka virtual platform). This is the foremost thing you need to do when you start your meeting, introduce yourself, introduce everyone present, and then move on to explaining the agenda for your meeting. These 3 simple steps grab everyone's attention and help them have a clear vision, of the meeting. Essentially, at the end of these 3 steps, everyone in the meeting will be on the same page and ready to begin.

Give people things to do

This should be easy because you have already thought about why and how your attendees can contribute to this meeting. Since you already know their capabilities and their roles, you can easily assign tasks for them to take care of. The task can be directly related to solving the issue or be as simple as taking follow-ups. No matter what, make sure everyone is involved and is actively contributing. Without this, most attendees will feel that the meeting was meaningless.

Use an ice-breaker

Well, if it's one of the first meetings with your team or there are fresh faces in the meeting, it's always best to use an ice-breaker. Allot the first 15 minutes of the meeting for this ice-breaker session. This can be a simple group activity that helps everyone get comfortable and get acquainted. This sets the tone of the meeting and also helps your members to work together as a team.

Follow up

It's common for leaders to conduct a meeting when there is an emergency and completely forget about it. That's not a great practice for the efficiency of your team and your team members' morale. Always have a definite time when a follow-up will happen. You can also schedule separate follow-ups for different elements of the meeting. If you feel it's too much for you to take on, select members from the meeting who will solely be responsible for taking follow-ups and reporting to you.

Check out action items in progress

It's a great exercise to have a checklist based on the agenda, of the meeting. Before the meeting begins, have this checklist on the screen. At the end of the meeting, check out items from the list. This will imbibe a sense of challenge in your team members and pique their interest in the meeting.

Well, that may seem like, a lot of work, but the more you implement these steps in practice, the faster this "drill" of meeting etiquettes, will come naturally to you.

Now, you are clear on what you need to do during remote meetings, but it's equally important for your attendees to be sure of what they can expect from the meeting. Until everyone is in tandem, about the what, why, and when, you can't expect a meeting to be successful.

Creative networking ideas for virtual events

Since you will be conducting virtual events more frequently than in-person ones, here are some ideas to help you organize these events (Palmer, 2021):

- A pre-event photo contest: your virtual event can have a theme, and participants can be asked to enter a photo contest (with exciting prizes for the winners). This will get them excited about the event and make them feel involved.

- Coffee talk: a good way to turn a regular meeting into a casual, interactive event is coffee talk. Arrange the event during the usual coffee time and ask participants to interact with each other while sipping on coffee. This immediately changes the tone of the meeting to something more relaxed and casual.
- Break-out rooms: if you want to mix it up during regular meetings, too, organize break-out rooms where participants are randomly put into smaller groups for 10-15 minutes where they can interact among themselves.
- In-house entertainment: lighten things up by including performances by musicians and artists for the event. They can perform live on screen or send their videos pre-recorded to be played during the event.

Best online meeting tools

If your head is already bursting with ideas, here are some online meeting tools that you can use to implement these ideas (May 2020)-

- Zoom: Widely used all over the world. This is free software but has a subscription version as well with added features. You can share screens, and documents, customize backgrounds, and organize break-out rooms here.
- Skype Meet Now: This version of Skype is flexible and can be used to connect with people who have skype profiles and those who won't.

Skype meet now has all the features of the original skype.
- Google Meet: Google meet is easy to use, easy to schedule, and collaborative. You can share screens and work together while on google meet.
- Google Hangouts: Google hangouts also allows group video calls for people using it free of cost. Not too many collaborative features, but it does the job.
- GoToMeeting: This collaborative platform has a 14-day trial period which you can check out. The paid version has unlimited up time and participant load.
- Bluejeans: This is a cloud-based collaborative platform with enhanced features like real-time translations.
- Cisco Webex meetings: This cloud-based platform provides online meetings with HD audio and video quality and can host up to 100 people.

Here is what information you should put in a virtual meeting invite

- Concise subject line

The subject line shouldn't be too long. Too many adjectives and words will only confuse the invitees about what the meeting is being called for. Keep it concise- not more than 7-10 words at maximum. Don't use too many technical terms that can confuse people. The best practice is to include the "what" of the meeting here.

- Personal introduction

No one really bothers to include this in the invite, and this may harm the turn-out of the meeting. People need to know who is calling the meeting to be aware of who they will be listening to for maybe an hour. The attendees will give their time to this meeting, and hence they should know with whom they will be primarily engaging.

- Preparation requirements

To boost the productivity of any meeting, it's best to mention in the invite preparations needed from the attendees. For example, if they need to provide certain data since the last meeting, or have their notes ready, and so on. This ensures that all attendees have already geared up for the meeting.

- Meeting date and time

As obvious as it is, the meeting date and time is the most important part of the invitation. Make sure you mention the time in a common time zone or multiple time zones if required. Cross-check both the time and date before sending the invite to avoid any mix-up.

- Location and medium

In the case of remote meetings, the location doesn't

matter, but if you mention the location, people will know what time zone you're in (in case they are confused about the time). The links attached with the invite do not always clearly reflect the medium used. Thus, it's best to mention the medium: Skype, Google Meet, Zoom, and so on, so that the attendees can set up the software if they don't have it.

- Meeting objective

Below the subject line, there should be one or two sentences about the meeting objective. This will inform the attendees about the content of the meeting. The objective is the same as the checklist you will have for the meeting, just in a brief format.

- Agenda

Well, the agenda and objective may seem similar, but they are not. However, your attendees will surely need both the information to clearly understand the meeting. The objective of the meeting is the issue that is to be resolved, whereas the agenda is the greater "why" of the meeting. Include things like how this meeting will contribute to the company's growth in the agenda.

If you maintain this format for sending your remote meeting invites, you can expect your meetings to go smoothly and have the expected outcomes.

But there is another crucial element to any meeting, whether in-person or remote: note taking. There needs to be a system in place to note the minutes of the meeting. Without the minutes, it's impossible to keep track of the key takeaways of the meeting mentally.

How you can make the best meeting notes in remote meetings

- Start with the basics

Basics work the best for your meetings. Try using a simple pen and paper or the online google docs for meeting minutes. This should work for small-scale meetings where there aren't too many spokespersons.

- Verbatim transcript

For large-scale meetings with several speakers and presenters, using verbatim transcript software is the best. It may cost you additionally, but it will give you the unfiltered and accurate written word for all that is said in the meeting. A verbatim transcript software is a good way to keep the details in point.

- Filter down to key points

That's why notes, are called notes, they are ideally brief, written simply in points that capture the gist of the discussion. A good note mentions all the key points without fail while keeping the irrelevant information off the record.

If you feel overwhelmed about conducting the meeting and keeping track of the minutes, identify someone in your team who has good diligence and hand them this task. In any case, never skip note-taking during meetings as, it can hamper the final impact of the meeting.

This is all that you should keep in mind about

conducting remote meetings for your teams. However, if you are ambitious and want your business to grow steadily, you can step up your game using "networking events". Networking events are common for companies of any scale to promote better working relationships.

You're wrong if you think that for businesses on the virtual platform networking events don't apply. Networking events can be very beneficial in boosting your team's integrity and growing your business overall.

But, what exactly are networking events?

Networking events are one-five day events organized for people in the network marketing business. These events consist of successful network marketers' talks on various aspects of network marketing. Now, it may sound like a boring conference meant for school kids to learn, but it's everything but that. Networking events are the best opportunities to interact, grow your network, and find better clientele (Author, 2021). Let's objectively look at why networking events are important for networking marketing businesses.

- Stay updated on recent trends

Networking events gather network marketers all over the globe. By listening to their approach to their businesses, you will get a better idea of the successful trends in network marketing and what works and what doesn't. This knowledge is not available in any other way.

- Connect with people who are otherwise far fetched

Networking events are a great way of interacting with people you aspire to be, with leaders of the network marketing industry. While on social media, they may or may not notice your reaction to their posts, they will surely interact with you in network marketing events because that's what they are here for.

- Promote your business

When promoting your business online, you're never sure how many people it has reached and how many genuinely engage with your posts. In-person networking events are a great way to meet like-minded people and make them aware of your business: even simply exchanging business cards will make them take notice of you.

- Build better working relationships

There are many collaborators that you can get through these events. By interacting with people and exchanging ideas and opinions, you develop your own space in the network marketing "clan" thereby building new and better working relationships with others in the field.

- Get inspired and develop ideas

Networking events are expected to have certain talks and testimonials where successful people share their journeys in this field. This can be very inspiring and replenish your zeal if you've been running low on it.

You can attend such networking events to position yourself into the network marketing community or organize these events to help promote and grow your business. Either way, networking events are extremely beneficial if you want to stay in network marketing, in the long run.

Importance of destination events in network marketing: you may feel that it's a lot of hassle to travel around to attend these destination events. You may not be keen on spending the time, money, or effort to attend these. That's what differentiates successful leaders from forever aspiring leaders in this field: persistence. You must persistently attend these events, one after the other, if you want to grow. According to statistics, those who keep attending these events make twice the average of anyone else in the room, and after some time, you will become one of the top earners, in the industry.

Why does this work? Because the information, the inspiration, and the connections shared, in these events are exclusive. No other virtual meetings can provide you the same. These networking events are the inside track of the network marketing industry. It is very important to persistently attend these and collaborate actively to place yourself in the industry's top tier.

- Making destination retreats with your team member

This is a secret tip that I have held on to for too long. Destination retreats with your team members are a common occurrence in most companies. The secret is who all are included in this retreat. A very important aspect, as most companies invite everyone on the team and just enjoy work-free time, over the weekend, or so. If you want to successfully grow your business, you need to diverge a little bit. So before planning these retreats, make sure that you have identified your top team members, the ones who are bringing you the numbers, making sales, and working diligently throughout (even if they belong to the 5% ers).

Gather all these selected individuals for a Thursday through Sunday retreat. Keep the first day for team activities and amazing lunches. From the second day onwards, sneak in small sessions of "leadership training" and "bonding sessions". This will allow you to harness the potential of the best members of your team and inspire them to do better. In summary, you need to put in the extra effort for those who are working efficiently to keep your company moving ahead. (Robbins, 2019).

How in-person and virtual events can co-exist

If you are currently confused about which way to boost your business: virtual networking events or in-person networking events, the best way is both (Blohm, 2022).

However, you must be mindful while combining the best of these worlds. There are certain factors you need to keep in mind.

- When to use what

For this, you need to know your audience. You can choose an in-person meeting for high-profile clients and larger deals and virtual meetings to connect with existing clients to answer their queries.

- Costing

Well, organizing or traveling to networking events involves a lot of investment, whereas remote meetings don't. Thus, you have to do the math, before you get all excited and want to throw a large-scale networking event. Make sure your investment doesn't exceed your profits.

- Balance

It's important to find the perfect balance of organizing virtual meetings and in-person events such that the returns from those don't cancel each other out. My advice, would be to use networking events sparingly, compared to remote meetings. However, think through the requirements of both, before making any decisions.

Key points:

- Virtual meetings have numerous advantages, such as cost reduction, boosting productivity, global reach, and more
- Virtual meetings require less effort than in-person meetings but need some effort, nonetheless
- It is also important to attend in-person networking events to help your business grow
- At present, the ideal way to make your business

successful is by combining virtual events and in-person networking events, to help your business grow
- Make sure the what, why, and when of any meeting is clear to you as well as conveyed to the participants

You have covered enough ground to understand and start building an efficient team, from your enthusiastic new enrollees, and to get the engine running. It's high time to revert to your original motivation behind starting this business, making money! It's common to forget all about it when you're focused on getting prospects and building business relationships. To know how to get the profits rolling into your business, tune into the next chapter.

By the way, if you are enjoying this book, remember to leave a review in amazon. For instructions, go to page 143.

8

Becoming the Online Merchant

We are almost at the end of your journey to step in and lead the virtual marketing world. It's important to look back, on things. This chapter is about looking back and tying the loose ends. Remember why you began this journey, in network marketing in the first place? If not, take a moment and close your eyes and remind yourself. What was your basic aim? Be sure to be as honest and transparent as possible.

I assume that for most of you, the answer is, making money. Indeed, there is nothing selfish about that. You aim to make money through networking marketing and leading a network marketing team, that is why you are here, now, at the last few pages of this book.

Maybe, through all the previous chapters talking about team building, training enrollees, and signing up prospects, the primary aim (money-making) had taken a back seat. Yes, you still need to ace all these intermediary steps to ultimately achieve your primary aim. At this point, in your journey, where you have already taken care of your team's functioning and organization, presented your products or services, created awareness about your brand, and made reasonable follow-ups. Now is the time to make conversions and make money.

You may think that since all the intermediary goals are already crossed off your list, the last part- making sales and generating money, should be easy. Let me tell you, it's anything but that. This is because, in this world, not every great leader is a great businessperson and vice versa. Leading people and making a profit from your business, are two very different ball games. So, even if you feel confident about all the team building and interaction, for your business, you need to concentrate on the strategies that will ultimately help you make money.

This chapter is all about achieving virtual sales and expanding the network marketing business, online. Make sure you adopt the tips and tricks, in this chapter to your business setting, and not just blindly follow the steps. Also, start implementing these steps, immediately, undergo trials and errors, and modify the strategies, if required. At this point, you have to play the field to start seeing those sales numbers, go up.

This chapter is thoughtfully designed, to help you through all the steps of expanding your network marketing business and, is filled with strategies, derived from real-life experiences to help you make those virtual sales.

Step One: Generating Sales Leads

The following steps discuss how you can get leads to make sales and expand these leads with time (Tyre,2021).

Identify target audience

If you already haven't done this, you must do it now. Be conscious about whom you are trying to sell your product to. This will ensure a higher probability of making the sale and save you time and effort from approaching the wrong person. If you have a Facebook group, or an Instagram page for your business, check out what your followers comprise of. Get to know them, use the daily method of operation and engage with your audience. It's crucial to know what kind of life your audience has, and what age group they fall in; mostly to identify the "pain points".

Remember, how to use "pain points" for virtual marketing? Use these pain points to bond with your audience and then pitch your product. Following these steps and having background knowledge about your audience will increase your chances of making a sale exponentially.

Pick promotional methods wisely

We have already covered multiple different ways in which you can promote your product. But, what we haven't covered is the selection of the promotional method. Yes, you cannot just use any method according to your wish. If you do that, it won't get you anywhere. You need to be wise- choose your promotional method wisely.

After knowing your audience, take a few days to track what appeals to your audience the most. Is it videos, live streams, or blog posts? Where do you get the maximum engagement? Now, choose your promotional method for this assessment. If you find two or more methods working for your audience, alternate between these methods each week and mix them up to keep your audience engaged.

Create a sales funnel

This is essentially a top-down method of gathering information from your audience. This method can also be used to achieve the previous step and the next step in this list. Here, you try to gather general knowledge about your audience from a pool of people engaging in your group or posts.

You should have a dedicated form they can fill out when they visit your website: name, age, location, and occupation. Most people will not fill out this form because it takes time and effort. So, you need to provide some initiative, a discount code, early access to some information, letting them in on an exclusive group related to the product, and so on.

Assemble all the information in a Customer Relations Management (CRM) platform and track it over time to plan your marketing strategies.

Use an email newsletter to build relationships

This is a method that almost every business applies, no matter the scale of the business. This is because it works without fail. Most people who engage in your business page and social media accounts will do so only once. People tend to get busy and forget about things easily. A newsletter is a great way to remind them about your business and show them what they miss out on. Have pictures and clickable links to attract them to your business page. Note: remember to follow the regulations of the CAN-SPAM act.

Revisit closed/lost opportunities

While connecting with your audience and finding prospects, there will be many lost cases. This is the absolute truth. But you can surely use these lost cases to increase your leads later on. Revisit them and try to reconnect. To do this later, you first need to have notes about what went wrong during the first attempt. When you revisit them, ensure you have addressed or taken care of whatever went wrong initially. Politely reconnect with them without spamming their inbox, and try your luck, again. For many, the second or third time's the charm!

Ask current customers for referrals

This strategy works most of the time. The success rate will vary, but it increases your network nonetheless. Use your CRM data to identify clients who have been consistently engaging and purchasing from you. Send an email, direct message or call them for a quick chat and begin by thanking them for the business. Enquire whether they are satisfied with your products or not, and address any grievances they may have. If their response is on the positive side, ask them for any individuals or companies who may be interested in your service and try to get their emails, phone numbers, or social media handles.

This simple step will give you at least one lead from each phone call. Don't forget to offer your consistent clients some discounts or thank you notifications, from time to time. Make them feel valued. This increases their probability of referring your products, to someone else (Gregory, 2021).

Leverage social media

With the actual hustle of carrying the business forward, leaders often forget to sharpen their primary tools from time to time. The social media profiles. For any virtual network marketing business, social media profiles are the gateway to making sales. Make sure that all the business profiles are updated with the most recent information, are on track with all audience comments and questions.

When people visit your profiles and see that there has been no recent activity, they assume that you are not serious about your business, we don't want that, do we?

Get interactive through blog posts or live chats

Maybe you get high engagement through sharing videos and posts, only. No matter the trend of engagement from your audience, this one strategy works the best- live chats and blog posts. Live chats keep people excited for the upcoming session, and the comment sections are a good place to keep the ball rolling, even after the live session, has ended.

On the other hand, blog posts (informative and personalized) help people connect with your product as well as give them relevant information for free, and people really appreciate it. So, no matter what, don't forget to use both these strategies for your marketing.

Host a webinar or workshop

This is a two-way street. Hosting a workshop for interested enrollees and prospects is effective in locking in the sales, and this profits your business. While for the prospects and enrollees themselves, it's a learning experience that helps them develop their knowledge base. Overall, this marketing strategy is a win-win situation.

Have a giveaway for a free product or service in exchange for lead

This strategy should be your safe bet. If you feel things are not working out, resort to this trick, and trust me, you will get back on track. Announce a free giveaway of a product if people tag at least 5 people on your product posts or ask 5 people to follow your page. The reason why this works like magic to expand your business, is that people inherently love gifts!

Partner with other businesses online to cross-promote your offerings

Find collaborators and engage with the audience

together. If your business is about a wellness product, partner with another wellness product business to promote your services together. Encourage the audience to use both the products together for the best results. This way, you can reach your audience as well as the audience of the other business. The single effort, double gains!

Step 2: Skyrocket Your Conversion Rate

Not all those who visit your website are successfully converted into customers all the time. The basic idea of making sales comes from high conversion rates. The more successful purchases you have, the higher the sales and profits. Here are ten ways to skyrocket your conversion rate effectively (Martins, 2022).

Add live chat

People visit your website for multiple reasons, maybe they are just bored and killing time, unsure of what your page is about, or genuinely interested in making a purchase. A live chat option that pops up on the page for every visitor is a great way to understand what the visitor is looking for and guide them in the direction of purchase.

This also appeals to the human psychology of accountability; once people have announced in the live chat that they are looking to make a purchase, they will mostly go through the purchase as they are now accountable.

Track visitor interactions

Knowledge is power, and it's true, in your marketing journey. The more you know how visitors interact with your site, the better you can modify things to convert visitors into customers. Use a tool like a website grader to understand at what point of their browsing visitors get stuck or leave the site without making a purchase. This will help you remove any element from your website that is hindering your conversion rate.

Have a virtual store in action

A virtual store is a great addition to your website. Make sure that the products are organized efficiently and are easy to spot. The virtual store should have a simple design and should be easy to navigate. Your aim should be to make the process from browsing the website to making the purchase smooth and as hassle-free as possible. Make sure you don't ask your customers to provide unnecessary information or ask them to fill up long forms before they checkout the item. The design of the virtual store should encourage them to purchase in the shortest amount of time possible. People usually don't like to spend both time and effort together. Save their time, effort and increase your sales.

Use a CRO planner

CRO planners are software or cloud-based sites that help you analyze your website such that you can improve your website elements. Connecting your website with a CRO planner will enable you to track visitor interactions, understand trends and conduct different tests for website assessments that lead to progressive modifications. If you don't bother with this, you will never understand why your conversion rate is stuck at one point. Sales expansion is difficult without real-time data and tracking (Praill, 2022).

Include social proof

As per statistics, 89% of customers check your product's or website's reviews before visiting your site. This is an integral part of your business's reputation, and it connects to the conversion rate. No visitor will trust buying products from your website if they don't have socially viable proof of your product's efficacy. Thus, have reviews listed on your website or link your website to a platform where customers have left reviews, for your product (Riserbato,2022). These reviews should also be shared through your Facebook Group to make people aware of the positive effects of your product. It's ultimately the Facebook group from which you can reach the maximum number of people after all.

Conduct A/B testing

This is another part of tracking and gathering knowledge about your visitor interactions. The A/B testing method is a trial and error method whereby you try out different combinations and website outlay to understand which one works, for your audience. To conduct this testing, your website needs to be connected to a CRO planner.

Increase trust while removing any friction

Visitors will leave your site within 1 minute if your site isn't well maintained and spammy. With multiple untrustable links and outdated information popping up here and there, your site has no appeal to a visitor. You can very well forget about the conversion rate if this is the case. Thus, eliminate any unwanted links and elements that increase friction between your product and your visitors' purchasing will. Make the browsing experience smooth and enjoyable for the visitors.

Have a sales funnel

A sales funnel visualizes your website's conversion process for turning visitors into customers. There are the following stages- awareness, consideration, preference, purchase, loyalty, and advocacy. It's called a funnel because it's wider at the top, meaning most people will be aware, but fewer people will reach the advocacy stage. Track how your visitors move through each stage of the process, and at which stage they get stuck. Focus on the stages which see the least amount of audience.

For example, if you have enough customers but most aren't purchasing again, that is, most don't reach the loyalty stage, maybe you should conduct a satisfaction survey with those customers to find out why this is happening (Santora, 2020).

Pay-per-click campaigns

This method will allow you to increase your reach. You can collaborate with certain websites by asking them to include your product links. You need to pay for these websites on a per-click basis. The more clicks, the more you need to invest; however, the more prospective customers will be visiting your website. If all is well with your website and there's no friction, you can be assured that each click will convert to a purchase.

Contact forms

Include contact forms on your website. Ask visitors to leave their names and email IDs to stay updated with the latest offers, events, and your periodic newsletter. In this way, you can utilize the "lost opportunities," and those who are not sure at present about making a purchase, can be contacted later, on to try and convert them into customers.

Step 3: Making a successful virtual sale

Now that you know all about optimizing your website and enhancing visitors' browsing experience, you need to know how to successfully make sales through virtual platforms. This is the predominant aim, to surely make that sale and earn that sale. So, make sure you are implementing most of these strategies, if not all of them.

Attract qualified leads

All the leads you gather through your marketing can be categorized into three types: warm, cold, and qualified leads. For guaranteed sales, focus on the qualified leads first: these are the people who are genuinely interested in your product, have the budget to afford it, and have shown substantial interest in purchasing. Maybe their numbers are low, but each will get you a definitive sale. Thus, prioritize definite sales, first. Then move on to the warm leads: these are the people who have shown some interest, in your product. They have left their email id addresses or phone numbers, on your contact form, and have engaged with your posts. Approach these people next. According to statistics, 50% of these leads will convert to a sale.

And then, finally, approach your cold leads. These people may or may not have shown interest and may or may not have the budget or will to make the purchase. You would need to call 100 of them, to make one sale. Thus, this time-consuming category should be your last priority (Lares, 2020).

Plan your touchpoints

Prepare before you contact your leads. Note down their information and their preferred time to be contacted. Also, maintain a calendar with scheduled call or email to get in touch when needed. Make sure that you are aware of their preferences, the products they are interested in, and associated details. Make a prior decision about whether you want to contact them via email or video call. In summary, be prepared to handle these sales calls; an unprepared and rushed call will only confuse your prospect and turn them off.

Monitor and learn from buyer interactions

As mentioned in the previous step, you need to use the data from your buyer interactions to make sales effectively. Thus, before you plan your marketing strategy to make the virtual sale, go through your buyer interaction data and prepare likewise. For example, track how long it takes a buyer to make a purchase finally, or during virtual meetings, track your prospect's facial expressions to gauge what is working and what is not.

Share presentations materials before you sign on

This is how you go the extra mile to successfully make a virtual sale and close a deal. When arranging virtual meetings with your clients, share the presentation material with your clients beforehand. This will give them a clear idea of what to expect from the meeting and also get them interested in the content. This is an extra effort but worth it (Factory, 2021).

Focus on building lasting business relationships

This is the ultimate secret of successful businesses. You need to build lasting relationships with your clients and business partners. Now, in the case of network marketing over virtual platforms, this is a challenge. The absence of personal presence immediately, reduces the tuning between you and your prospect. Thus, always take time and be patient: building strong business relationships over virtual platforms will take time and multiple interactions before you finally strike a balance.

Be authentic, even if you're not perfect

Maybe you forgot to dress up for a meeting, let it be. Sometimes, clients appreciate real-life struggles coming to the forefront. Finally, deliver, make sure you follow up when you're supposed to and are punctual for meetings. Without these values, you cannot expect to build any strong business relationships.

Be a problem solver

Virtual selling is often equated with being a traditional hawker in a market. At present, it's far from that. To successfully make virtual sales, you need to be a problem solver for your prospect. You need to engage with them and understand their problems while identifying all the problems your product can solve. Thus, essentially you are a solution-bearer for your clients. This will put you in a trustable position for your prospects. Remember, they need to trust you before they make the purchase and trust the product.

Have a strategic delivery plan

You must say the right things at the right time to ensure your prospect is engaged. First, you need to take time and understand their problems; second, while being a problem solver, you need to have a strategic delivery. This means you need to combine the right proportions of educational content with customer statistics and genuine information to convince your prospect, to make the purchase. Opt for strategic deliveries like this rather than nagging your prospect to buy the product.

Get yourself a mentor and a partner

It can become very overwhelming to go through this selling process, and you may feel disappointed if things don't work out. For all of it, it's best to have a sales partner and a sales mentor. A sales partner should be someone at the same stage of virtual selling as you are, while a sales mentor should be someone with 3-7 years of experience in the field. Make up a sales team with these people and work, in tandem, to get results without experiencing burnout.

Buddy up with marketing

Realistically speaking, it's ultimately your marketing team engaging with prospects, creating blog posts, shooting out cold emails, and creating awareness about the product. Include your marketing team to devise a sales plan or resolve any sales crises. The marketing team is the most informed, about the product, and engages with audiences, daily. Their knowledge can help you enhance your sales plan, substantially.

Summary

Leading a team and making virtual sales to start making profits are two very different ball games. All the strategies listed in this chapter must be implemented ritualistically and assessed for success rates. You need to go through a lot of trial and error before you reach steady sales. Remember to track customer interactions, get preference data, and include the marketing team in creating a sales plan. Finally, you need to be flexible about the sales plan as, with time, trends tend to change, and so will the collective preference of your prospects. You need to keep up with your audience and modify your content accordingly to keep it relatable and appealing.

Key points:

- Know your target audience, have clean and

professional social media handles and apply sales strategies to generate leads.
- Track visitor interactions, and use CRO Planners and information databases to shoot up your conversion rates.
- Focus on building relationships, deliver strategically and work in a team to make successful virtual sales.

Coming up:

There exists a space where you can combine all your efforts of team building, recruitment, finding leads, and making sales to get your business up and about. To know what this space is and how you can use it, tune into the next chapter.

9

Social Selling for Your Team

Do you realize that you have already left the storm far behind? And you have managed to keep your team on the boat with you and sailed to the other side? Yes, that's how far we have come.

Now, believe it or not, we are at the last leg of this journey. Through the last eight chapters, I have shared with you the top secret strategies of this industry. Now, it is time for the final one. So, hold on to your chairs, and read on.

The whole aim of this book was to make you a virtual leader in the network marketing industry. The truth is network marketing in today's world is led by those who know how to harness the power of social media platforms. Without utilizing social media features, you cannot scale heights, in this field. You may already be a pro on social media, or you may be a complete newbie. No matter which, social media for network marketing is completely a different arena.

Even though I have already dedicated parts of this book to social media, for network marketing, it has been in bits and pieces. This time, it's a full chapter that tells you the best ways of using social media platforms for everything related to your business: getting leads, training your leaders, marketing and sales. It's a single, powerful tool for growing all aspects, of your business.

As per statistics, nearly 50% of top leaders use social media tools to train their team members and build their businesses even stronger. It's the digital age, and if you want to survive, it's imperative to get accustomed to the social media way of doing business.

No matter your current know-how and fluency, in using social media, for your business, you will know all the tricks that exist at the end of this chapter. This chapter discusses how you can leverage social media in various ways, from training your associates to boosting your sales to building a strong online network marketing business.

But first, what is social selling?

Social selling is the strategy of using various media platforms to grow your business (Baker, 2020). This growth is multilinear and includes generating awareness, adding opportunities and prospects, and active collaboration to extend your network pipeline. This is the basic method you need to implement at every stage of your business but with different intensities.

When starting your business, you would need to follow guidelines to the letter to see some progress. At the intermediary stage, you need to start modifying the guidelines, to fit the direction of your business. Finally, when your business reaches steady growth, you still need to apply these strategies wisely, to help your business maintain its position while aiming for more profits.

Why is it important?

Social selling expands your opportunities like no other. All over the world, there are approximately 3.6 billion people who actively use social media. All these people are your prospects, and social media creates the space for you to turn these prospects into clients. If you isolate your business from social media, you will lose access to this global pool of prospects. A substantial portion of this book has already dealt with ways to use social media to make virtual sales, interact with your clients, and convert prospects into clients. Using social media correctly to achieve your business' small and large goals is unparalleled. Your business will never become irrelevant to people if you consistently engage through social media.

What is not social selling?

The tricky part of social selling is not about understanding what it is. Rather, it's about what it isn't (Rowley, 2017). More often than not, people think that social selling is the equivalent of social marketing for your business: that's completely incorrect. So, to strengthen your understanding of social selling, you must first know what social selling isn't (aka strategies you shouldn't mix up with social selling strategies).

- It isn't outsourcing to marketing

Since social selling is based on creating awareness about your business through social media, most people confuse this with digital marketing. Social selling is beyond marketing strategies. It's about connecting to prospects and clients and creating interpersonal relationships that increase sales probabilities. So, while building a social selling strategy, train your team to build awareness on social media.

- It isn't about automation

If you feel that sharing your business-related content on social media by just automating posts and sharing via your team member's social media profiles: you are wrong. Automated sharing and resharing feel unauthentic and rarely grab their attention. Avoid automating posts and shares if you want to have an impact, on your audience. Instead, try adding personal comments, thoughts, or relatable quotes while resharing the post to make it more interesting.

- It isn't a one-time event

Social selling isn't effective when it's nothing more than sudden jolts of activities followed by a long period of inactivity. You shouldn't make social selling a one-time event. Most people mistake being active, on their business pages only, when a product launch is coming up, or the sales aren't great. This approach has almost no effect on your revenue. Social selling is effective only when one is consistent. Daily efforts into social media management for your business will show up as profits gradually.

- It isn't immediate

Picking up from the last line of the previous point, social selling isn't immediate. If you expect your sales to grow after being active for only one day, you will be hugely disappointed. Social selling is a cumulative process that compounds its results with every day that you commit to it. Immediate results are just not a part of social selling.

- It ain't modern trickery

One can adopt many approaches for moving ahead with social selling. Trickery shouldn't be one of them. No matter how desperate you are to make that sale, you should focus on building genuine relationships with your prospects. Quick and easy trickery is never going to work.

- It isn't the new channel for spam

Speaking of desperation, yes, it's normal to be desperate about earning profits. But this doesn't justify spamming your prospects' inboxes without any consideration. Social selling is about the right balance and restraint wherever required, blended with the right amount of approaching strategies. You need to understand the line between approaching your prospects and spamming them with content.

- It isn't cold calling

Cold calling is a common marketing strategy to get cold leads and make at least one sale among hundreds. Applying the same strategy to social selling takes the fun out of the entire process and doesn't give you any results. Cold calling should be kept far away from your social selling plan.

- It isn't replacing face-to-face interaction

Nope, you can't avoid in-person interactions forever. No matter the virtual nature of your business, sales can and should be done, offline, whenever the opportunity presents itself. A good salesperson has selling skills on social media as well as during face-to-face interactions.

- It isn't magic

You can't expect social selling to be your magic solution for low sales. Low sales can result from multiple gaps in the product or service itself. Social selling won't fill those gaps. Thus, use social selling strategies and enhance your services to make those sales.

- It isn't stalking

As mentioned before, you must be well within the lines while approaching your prospect. While trying to build business relationships online, don't start stalking your prospects and start over-interacting with them 24 X 7. This won't result in a sale, but your profile will get reported.

- Doesn't replace phones and email

Social selling is also not a replacement for sales through calls and emails. Instead, all these methods must be applied in tandem to see considerable results. Don't forget about good old sales calls and newsletters while pouring your energy into social selling.

- It isn't about media

You are mistaken if you think having a social media profile or business page is enough for social selling. You need to use social media actively to network and find leads and collaborations.

- It may not be for everyone

This is something you need to consider before you move ahead with social selling. You must know your target audience and also gauge whether the majority of them are on social media or not. If they aren't, then you don't need social selling. Be where your buyers are, simple.

Pros and cons of using social media

Like everything in this world, social media has two sides: the good and the not-so-good. You need to be fully aware of the pros and cons of social media for business before you decide to move ahead with social selling (Ward, 2020).

Pros

- Free of cost or low cost: having a social media account for your business doesn't cost anything. It's free to use, and it will help you make sales. In cases where there is some cost involved, if you opt for premium versions of some social media

platforms, but compared to the networks you will build, the cost is minimal.
- Direct management with customers: it's a hassle-free way to stay connected with your customers. Social media handles are also used as customer support, by some businesses, and it has been a successful way of managing your customers' queries. Thus, you can efficiently take care of the most hectic part of the business (customer management) via your social media profile.
- Able to learn more about customers: when you connect with your prospects and customers through social media, you get to know about their lives. You will be able to gain insight into their problems and brainstorm ways in which your product can help them. This knowledge makes your sales strategies more effective.

Cons

- Time-intensive: well, for social selling to be effective, you need to be active every day. You need to be available for long periods to connect with different customers (sometimes across time zones) and make your sales pitches. Thus, it is a time-intensive method without any fixed breaks or signing-off time.
- Direct advertising is less effective: when you use social media for your business, direct selling won't work. The audience won't be interested if you only talk about selling your product. You need to create engaging content and make it a

step-by-step process toward a sale. Direct selling strategies are not meant for social media.
- Increases risk of public criticism and hacking: certain risks are involved when you share your business content with the public via social media. Among all the people who view and engage with your content, hackers may misuse your business information. You should also expect to face some criticism or negativities from the audience in general. This is part and parcel of social selling (S., 2022).

Popular social media platforms for business

Now that you know what exactly social selling is and isn't and are aware of the pros and cons of social media for business, you must have decided for your business. If you decide that your business does have a considerate audience on social media platforms, here are 5 places where you can connect with them:

- YouTube

It's a popular platform that the most people, use all across the globe. You can create engagement for your business through videos, periodically. The videos may be promotional for your products or simply about various aspects of your business. You can also build a youtube community and keep them tuned in via posts or blog write-ups even when you don't post videos for a long time. The youtube comment section can also become a good place for connecting with your subscribers.

- Facebook

According to a recent survey, 69% of social media users globally are on Facebook. Thus, Facebook can be your gateway to a global customer base. You can build a Facebook page for your business and keep it updated with posts, videos, customer testimonials, and more. You can also create an exclusive Facebook group (already covered in a previous chapter) to build a community of people interested in your business.

- Instagram

Instagram is the second most widely used social media platform at present. Many businesses have boomed through their Instagram pages only. However, the content for your Instagram business page needs to be well-groomed since the competition is steep. You can engage with your audience via live chat, polls, and reels related to your business.

- LinkedIn

LinkedIn is a more professional space than all the other social media platforms. Your business page on LinkedIn needs to be very professional looking and neat, to attract quality leads. Engagement on LinkedIn can be created through blog posts and direct messages. There are also dedicated sections to share your business licenses, certifications, and other achievements, this boosts the reputation and transparency of your business. LinkedIn is a great platform to build and expand your business network.

- WhatsApp

There exists a version of WhatsApp called "WhatsApp business" that can be used to engage with customers. You can list your products in the Whatsapp profile and also automate messages to deal with customer inquiries. However, your WhatsApp number should be linked to your website or other social media handles for people to reach out to. We recommend using WhatsApp, along with other social media platforms, for social selling.

Using social media for training your team

As you can gauge from the previous sections, social selling is a tricky method and your leaders need to be trained to implement the strategies, successfully. Here is how you can train your team to use social media for sales (Baker, 2020) -

- Inform them about the 3 C's of social media

Context, content, and collaboration are the three essential Cs of social selling. Your team leaders must be well versed in these three, to make sales successfully. They should first create a context, in their profile, and state it clearly: who they are, what's the purpose of their profile, and what they offer. Next, they must develop engaging content relevant to your business, which works for their audience. Finally, they should build collaborations through effective engagement with the audience. These are prerequisites of social selling and ensure that your team members are well trained.

- Make sure your team leaders have a strong social media profile

Choose members from your team who already stand well on social media platforms, they should have a respectable number of subscribers/ followers/ networks. This provides the basis for moving ahead with social selling. For any team member who doesn't have influence on social media platforms, it will be difficult to garner attention and get leads.

- Encourage your team members to have sales goals

This is how you scale up your social scales. Each leader responsible for social selling should have a weekly or monthly, sales target. This will push them to remain active and work consistently towards making those sales.

- Encourage your team leaders to nurture rep-to-prospect connections

They need to know the correct way of engaging with their prospects. They should strive to develop well-balanced interpersonal relationships with their prospects to increase the conversion rate. Your team leaders should go beyond creating content, being active on social media platforms, and nurturing healthy connections with the audience.

- Make sure they know the target audience

Well, none of the last four steps will work if your team

leaders don't know their audience. They should be targeting the correct set of audiences, for your business. Engaging with people who don't relate to your business, would be a waste of time. Thus, your leaders should implement all the strategies to a targeted audience, for your business, rather than everyone.

Summary

Social media is the ultimate tool, in the virtual network marketing industry. No matter your business type, you will always find people, online, who would be interested in it. Globally, 3.6 billion people are active on social media. Social selling is the method of making and increasing your sales via social platforms. Social selling should not be confused with social marketing. Your teammates should be taking the lead in social selling. They should be trained in the three C's (context, content, and collaboration) to make social sales, successfully. There is a line between spamming, stalking, and social selling. Your team leaders need to strike the correct balance between approachability and restraint, while engaging with prospects, online. There are multiple social media platforms with distinctive features where you can begin with social selling for your business, just make sure that your target audience is also present, on that social platform.

Key points

- Social selling is an essential way of making profits in your business

- Social selling is important to create a network, generate leads, and increase your conversion rate.
- Use the 3 C's of social selling to make it simple for others to do.
- Your team members should be trained before they begin social selling.
- Your team should have a good social media presence to make sales successfully.

Conclusion

Whether you're a beginner in network marketing or have already started sailing, you need to be aware of all the qualities a virtual leader should have. You may aim to be a leader or not but striving for these qualities will surely help you progress and achieve your goals, in network marketing. A successful virtual leader should develop the depth of their knowledge and read more books than average (>5) on a particular topic. They should also focus on their weak points and work on them, while restraining their strong attributes. To become a virtual leader, you must take action: implement the knowledge you gain through books in real-life settings. If you fail in an attempt, it's okay. Fail repeatedly, until failure doesn't scare you, anymore. Persistence and fearlessness are what you need to begin, this journey.

Another crucial aspect of success, in network marketing is nurturing interpersonal relationships. A good virtual leader must have excellent communication skills, body language, and positive energy. A successful leader is also coachable: you need to be willing to learn and adapt as time changes, and find solutions on, your own. Overall, at the beginning of your journey, you need to fine-tune your mindset to a leadership mindset and sharpen your soft skills.

Once you have trained yourself satisfactorily, you need to position yourself as an authority. That's how you will make yourself known, in the industry and people will gain interest in you and your business. Without accomplishing this step, it isn't possible to have any enrollees, prospects, or even kick start your network marketing business. You need to use social media platforms, at your disposal, to engage with people and identify, your target audience. Be active, approachable, and take an interest, in your audiences' lives.

Listen to them patiently and bond with them, before you even begin pitching, your business or product. During this phase of your journey, you need to be okay with the fact that enrollees are going to leave. Not everyone will stick around. In any case, you should know how to launch your enrollees, to the moon and keep them motivated, throughout. The more genuine enrollees you have, the more prospects you will gain, and the more your business will grow. At this stage, it's more important to be mindful about what you should avoid doing with your new enrollees than you should do. Not having unrealistic expectations from your enrollees is the best approach you can take during this time.

Now that you have enough people on board, you need to keep them on board. Chapters 5 and 6 are the best references to get through this stage. Make sure you focus on building a team culture rather than talking, business all the time. With so many people looking up to you as a leader, you would need to be vulnerable, from time to time. You

Conclusion

may believe it's counterproductive for a leader to be vulnerable, but that's not true. Your vulnerability, active listening, and genuine interest in your team members will make them feel valued, and without this feeling, they may leave.

Once you're sure of your team's organization and strength, you must move ahead full force and try to expand your business. Chapters 7 through 9 are full of strategies you need to apply to expand your network, increase your sales, retain loyal customers, and earn a good amount of profits. During this stage, it's important to stay focused and assess, and reassess the quality of goods and services you offer. Social media platforms (when used well) will elevate your marketing and sales. Be sure to engage the appropriate team for appropriate tasks such as sales for social selling and marketing for virtual engagement.

Finally, reassess your approach every few months, modify things, if required, and keep up with changing trends. Make sure that your marketing content is relatable, this way, your business will never go out of sales.

Takeaway:

- Train yourself to be a leader before you aim to train others
- Position yourself as an authority to start playing the field
- Engage actively with your prospects and train your enrollees to do so as well
- Keep up a positive team culture and encourage your team members through healthy competition and sales targets

Conclusion

- Use social media to expand your network and collaborate with others: this is how you double your reach.
- Make sure you and your team are not spamming or stalking people due to their desperation to make sales.
- Be focused, coachable and active over social media platforms as well as in in-person meetings.

Call to action:

- Make a list of all the skills you already have to begin your journey
- Make a plan of action for using social media platforms to leverage your business
- Find 3 ways through which you can improve your team's organization and performance.

The idea behind this book was to guide people who are lost. In today's world of non-stop hustle, people often struggle to keep up their pace and lose their direction. Fifteen years ago, we were exactly where you are, we couldn't see the path ahead of us at that time. After more than a decade of struggle, experience, and mentoring network marketers, we wanted to make all our strategies accessible to the masses. For many of you, this book might have become a guiding light for your virtual marketing journey, while for others, you may add more resources along with this book to upscale your position in the network marketing industry. In conclusion, if this book has helped

Conclusion

you get out of a rut, pace up or find direction in your network marketing journey, it sure has served its purpose.

Your feedback matters: If you enjoyed the book, please leave a review on Amazon. Turn to next page for steps on how to leave a review. Good luck on your network marketing journey!

Leave a Review

As an independent author, reviews are my livelihood on this platform. If you enjoyed this book, I'd really appreciate it if you left your honest feedback. You can do so by scanning the QR code with the camera in your phone. I love hearing from my readers and personally read every single review.

References

A. (2019, September 30). The Importance of Destination Events in Network Marketing. Network Marketing Pro. Retrieved July 28, 2022, from https://networkmarketingpro.com/the-importance-of-destination-events-in-network-marketing/

Author, B. (2021, October 25). Why Attending Networking Events Is Beneficial For Your Business. BAASS. Retrieved July 28, 2022, from https://www.baass.com/blog/why-attending-networking-events-is-beneficial-for-your-business

Baker, K. (2020, October 28). How to Train Your Team in Social Selling. Hubspot. Retrieved August 4, 2022, from https://blog.hubspot.com/sales/social-selling-training

Blohm, D. (2022, April 6). How In-Person And Virtual Events Can Co-exist In The Future Of B2B Marketing. Forbes. Retrieved July 28, 2022, from https://www.forbes.com/sites/forbescommunicationscouncil/2022/04/05/how-in-person-and-virtual-events-can-coexist-in-the-future-of-b2b-marketing/?sh=420be725d850

References

Cheng, A. (2022, March 10). 7 body language tips for your next video meeting. RingCentral. Retrieved June 24, 2022, from https://www.ringcentral.com/us/en/blog/7-body-language-tips-for-your-next-video-meeting/

Cummings, R. (2022). Dirtiest secret About network marketing. Street Directory. Retrieved June 30, 2022, from https://www.streetdirectory.com/travel_guide/147668/multi_level_marketing/dirtiest_secret_about_network_marketing.html

Everett, Z. (2020, June 9). Virtual Influencing - How to influence on Zoom. Zena Everett. Retrieved June 24, 2022, from https://www.zenaeverett.com/2020/06/09/virtual-influencing-how-to-influence-on-zoom/

Everything You Need to Know About Remote Meetings | Remote Work Guide. (n.d.). Wrike. Retrieved July 28, 2022, from https://www.wrike.com/remote-work-guide/remote-meetings-guide/

Factory, P. B. S. (2021, January 25). How to Successfully Make a Sale. Success Factory Blog. Retrieved August 3, 2022, from http://blog.successfactory.com/how-to-successfully-make-a-sale/

Gregory, A. (2021, September 13). How to Generate Sales Leads in Your Small Business. The Balance Small Business. Retrieved August 3, 2022, from https://www.thebalancesmb.com/how-to-generate-sales-leads-in-your-small-business-2951792

Higdon, R. [Network Marketing Systems and Duplication]. (2022, July 1). Facebook [Video]. Facebook. https://fb.watch/d_V33-XMsp/

Higdon, R. (2021, September 29). Network marketing team building | How To Keep Your Team From Feeling

References

Abandoned[Video]. YouTube. https://www.youtube.com/watch?v=a87RwHoklfw&feature=youtu.be

Higdon, R. (2021, September 14). How To Use Facebook Groups For Network Marketing. Video]. YouTube. https://www.youtube.com/watch?v=xUB0qPj2NQM

Higdon, R. (2020, May 12). Facebook - Ray Higdon [Video]. Facebook. https://m.facebook.com/rayhigdonpage/videos/2905368002852192/

Lares, A. (2020, December 10). How To Sell Virtually. Forbes. Retrieved August 3, 2022, from https://www.forbes.com/sites/forbescoachescouncil/2020/12/11/how-to-sell-virtually/?sh=1453e1fb359c

Martins, A. (2022, June 29). 9 Lead Conversion Tips For Success. Business.Com. Retrieved August 3, 2022, from https://www.business.com/articles/9-steps-to-lead-conversion-success/

May, T. (2020, April 22). 7 best video conferencing tools of 2020. Creative Bloq. Retrieved July 28, 2022, from https://www.creativebloq.com/features/video-conferencing-tools

Palmer, A. (2021, February 16). networking virtual events. Northstar Meetings Group. Retrieved July 28, 2022, from https://www.northstarmeetingsgroup.com/Planning-Tips-and-Trends/Event-Planning/Event-Programming/networking-virtual-events

Pousson, C. (2019, November 25). Network Marketing Success Tip: "Keep Them Around The Campfire". LinkedIn. Retrieved July 13, 2022, from https://www.linkedin.com/pulse/network-marketing-success-tip-keep-them-around-chuck-pousson-?fbclid=IwAR3nw1zNXGV0lcUNqb8a--7hYRniavhv2g-QI_SJNJp5eW3MvOBcLfEJYm6U

References

Premier on Demand. (2019, September 26). #1 How To Lead A Volunteer Team // Leadership 101 [Video]. YouTube. https://www.youtube.com/watch?v=pFXZA1G2GQI

Praill, D. (2022, June 30). Virtual Selling Techniques: 6 Best Ways to Engage Buyers and Increase Sales. VanillaSoft. Retrieved August 3, 2022, from https://vanillasoft.com/resource-center/blog/virtual-selling

Remote Team Meetings Guide | Boost Meeting Efficiency. (2020, March). Miro. Retrieved July 28, 2022, from https://miro.com/guides/remote-work/meetings

Riserbato, R. (2022, February 3). 20 Ways to Effectively Increase Your Conversion Rate. Hubspot. Retrieved August 3, 2022, from https://blog.hubspot.com/marketing/how-to-increase-conversion-rate

Rowley, J. (2017, February 1). What Social Selling Isn't. Hubspot. Retrieved August 4, 2022, from https://blog.hubspot.com/marketing/what-social-selling-isnt?_ga=2.216269270.1769321056.1601998466-331732295.1601998466

S. (2022, April 19). Managing and Leveraging Workplace Use of Social Media. SHRM. Retrieved August 4, 2022, from https://www.shrm.org/resourcesandtools/tools-and-samples/toolkits/pages/managingsocialmedia.aspx

Santora, J. (2020, August 14). 18 Proven Ways to Increase Your Sales Funnel Conversion Rate. OptinMonster. Retrieved August 3, 2022, from https://optinmonster.com/18-ways-increasing-conversions-throughout-your-sales-funnel/

Simone, M. (2020, October 20). How To launch a new

References

biz partner and team On social [Video]. Facebook. https://fb.watch/d_VaIRkEVB/

Simone, M. (2022, May 23).3 BIG Mistakes You Are Making In Your Facebook Group If You Want To Sell More. Video]. YouTube. https://www.youtube.com/watch?v=JAcAyr4k7Kk

Simone, M. (2021, July 22). How to Grow a Facebook Group FAST for your Network Marketing Business. Momsandheels.Com. Retrieved July 21, 2022, from https://www.momsandheels.com/42/?fbclid=IwAR2VFWAzJX4QQqTaK63FgosTXy21B-RdzJIfV8zNq01VbuLFhFdPjUt2_jM

Skousen, A. (2017, March 18). Top 5 Leadership Qualities Of A Network Marketing Leader. Have the Health, Business, and Life You've Always Dreamed Of. Retrieved June 24, 2022, from http://alyciaskousen.com/5-leadership-qualities/

Small Business Media Team 3. (2022, May 5). How to build personal relationships. SmallBusinessify.Com. Retrieved July 3, 2022, from https://smallbusinessify.com/how-to-build-personal-relationships/?fbclid=IwAR0vy3nH9mZYBzbDp3ZBI_E2RHK9ZGStrsdB5mUGxrIDdONfzGcZN6Xe7uw

Sorina, L. (2018, May 25). 12 Mistakes to Avoid in Facebook Groups. DRSOFT. Retrieved July 21, 2022, from https://drsoft.com/2018/05/25/mistakes-to-avoid-in-facebook-groups/?fbclid=IwAR1jbbt5haYUHfe46xqQkgurH2-qOVUsnsqK8uS-XlYt2Zf8Xnav3AVRlfY#schedule

Stevens, J. (2017, January 10). How To position yourself As A network marketing expert, even If you're brand new. Jenny Stevens. Retrieved June 30, 2022, from https://jen-

References

nystevenscoaching.com/blog/how-to-position-yourself-as-network-marketing-expert

The Network Marketers Den. (2021, May 13). Building relationships is the key factor for a successful network marketing business [Video]. YouTube. https://www.youtube.com/watch?v=A0Oy677va7k&feature=youtu.be

Tyre, D. (2021, April 13). How to Find Leads Online. Hubspot. Retrieved August 3, 2022, from https://blog.hubspot.com/sales/how-salespeople-can-generate-their-own-lead

Ward, S. (2020, September 21). What Is Social Network Marketing? The Balance Small Business. Retrieved August 4, 2022, from https://www.thebalancesmb.com/social-media-marketing-definition-2948527